PERSONA MEDUSA
A Tale of Selective Mutism & Social Anxiety

PERSONA MEDUSA
A Tale of Selective Mutism & Social Anxiety

D.J. Sharry

D.J. Sharry

2015

Some names have been changed in this book to protect the privacy of the people involved.

Cover Illustration

http://en.wikipedia.org/wiki/File:A_man_being_hunted_by_a_beast,_Bhimbetka_Cave_paintings.jpg#metadata by Raveesh Vyaas http://flickr.com/photos/32392356@N04 is licensed under CC BY – SA 2.0 http://creativecommons.org/licenses/by-sa/2.0/deed.en

Cover design by Logofvr

Copyright © 2015 by D.J. Sharry

All rights reserved. This book or any portion thereof may not be reproduced or used in any manner whatsoever without the express written permission of the publisher except for the use of brief quotations in a book review or scholarly journal.

First Printing: 2015

D.J. Sharry
Ashbourne, Meath, Ireland

Dedication

To my lovely wife Anita.
Thank you.

Contents

Acknowledgements ix

Preface xi

Introduction 1

▌ **C1: Head** 3

▌ **C2: Sick** 6

▌ **C3: Death** 10

▌ **C4: New Territory** 13

▌ **C5: Stepping on a Twig** 19

▌ **C6: Tiger Eyes** 23

◆ **C7: Camouflage** 25

◆ **T1: Shedding Coat** 34

◆ **T2: Twit Twoo** 36

◆ **T3: Clearing** 38

▬ **T4: Foraging** 42

▬ **T5: Open Defecation** 46

▬ **T6: Breaking Cover** 50

▬ **T7: Flickering Fires** 54

▬ **T8: Dominance** 56

- T9: Defending Territory 60
- T10: Masking Scent 66
- T11: Rickety Bridge 70
- T12: Wetlands 78
- L1: Cloud over Clearing 83
- L2: Greener Grass 87
- L3: Gatherer 93
- L4: Watering Hole 97
- L5: Hunter 102
- S1: Zombie 108
- S2: Attack 113
- S3: Death Roll 121
- S4: Blood Trail 123
- S5: Home 144
- C1: Tale End 151

Acknowledgements

I would like to thank Kristin Linklater for writing the extraordinary book 'Freeing the Natural Voice'.

Preface

My wedding was coming up. The choice of making a speech or not had been presented to me. I had decided to make a speech. I wanted to make a speech.

I had little over a year to prepare and the first thing I had to deal with was what happened to me when I first entered the school classroom at the age of four.

When I stood on that threshold an unmerciful torrent of anxiety rose up inside me and engulfed me whole.

I stopped speaking suddenly. For my thirteen years of school I was paralyzed. Since then my body has grown stronger and more able to contain the swipes and rips of the anxiety. By the time I made it into my twenties some sounds were even able to come out, though, I still would be known as the quiet one had I joined a monastery full of monks who had taken a vow of silence.

I had a safe area, home, which was the only place I could speak freely, but this safeness gradually became eroded by the immense anxiety that ate away at me in my away from home life.

I had often searched for a reason for that sudden stop sign in my life. If there was just a pinpoint of a bad thing that had happened then I could put my finger on it and deal with it but there was nothing very much out of the ordinary that happened in my first four years.

I had become accustomed to avoiding anything associated with not speaking, I would put down books when I came upon the word 'shy', would avoid any social event for dread of the word 'quiet'.

I then stopped and purposefully entered the term 'shyness' into an internet search engine, it threw up Selective Mutism.

I decided that for me to make that speech I would have to deal with the Selective Mutism issue in some way. I arranged to see a hypno-therapist.

The hypno-therapist brought me on a journey through my experiences so far in life. She spoke to me about being disconnected from my-self and the only way to reconnect was to feel these experiences again.

This book is an attempt to reconnect with my body and make peace with the anxiety by assigning my experiences a vertebra as I drop down my spine on a journey to my animal center in my sacral nerve plexi.

The spark of this book was ignited in the hypno-therapists room as I was stuck between the grinding stones of my past and future.

Introduction

Imagine you are walking through a savannah. You hear a low growl. You see a tiger burst out from the long grass. There is nowhere to run.

Our hero hears that low growl in every social situation and is standing in front of that tiger every time he is expected to speak. This millennia old survival mechanism gone awry is known as Selective Mutism.

Being mute in a social world, despite having the ability to speak, has led to puzzlement from people, some have attacked, some have befriended. Mostly our hero's life has run parallel to the intersecting lives of others but inevitably paths cross.

The memories of these crossings have become objects in our hero's head where his mind is stuck.

Our hero is getting married and is expected to give a wedding speech. He must deal with these objects and find his voice.

Our hero takes a journey out of his head. He travels down the vertebrae of his spine. Along the way he encounters these objects of obstruction which he looks back on through the imagined reflective pool in his pelvic basin. Each object is illuminated and slayed of their menace.

Our hero comes to rest at the base of his spine in the sacral nerve plexi, his animal instinctual center. He puts his arm around the stalking tiger and both predator and prey make peace with each other and unite.

Our hero steps up to make his speech.

Persona
That through which sound passes
Medusa
The terror that turns the onlooker to stone

⚑ C1: Head

I should go into the other room and say hello it's getting near finishing time I will have to get up and say goodbye that deadline there's time yet please don't ring I should ring a cup of tea no I might meet someone on the way to the kitchen staff meeting on Friday no no no were you at that meeting it's too late to go into the other room now wedding speech me that's ridiculous computer is shutting down I'll have to announce my departure now. 'Tlee you tomorrow'

I had to finish work on time to make it over for my appointment with my hypno-therapist. As I left my room I heard coming from the room across the hall computers shutting down, footsteps and rustling. My heart jumped into my mouth. I quickened my pace. I reached the stairs. I looked forward to the landing and turning the first corner. Their eyes could not see around corners. It would be like a shield on my back. I imagined them coming out of their room and not seeing me. I made it. I headed down the stairs quickly. I dropped my feet heavy on each step as a form of alarm bell to alert others of my coming. I heard movement and laughter on the ground floor. *How do they always have something to laugh about?* I slowed my pace. I hadn't been quick enough to make it out before the downstairs office. Now there was a delicate balancing act to perform. Too slow and those above would reach me and pass me. I would be expected to say something. Too fast and I'd bump into my colleagues from downstairs. I would be expected to say something. I heard them shouting and laughing and then the front door open and bang shut. *They're out.* I imagined them walking past the front of the building and turning the corner. I quickened my pace again. I heard my boss on the phone in the room across from the stairs. *It's the landline I'm safe there.* The footsteps behind me were getting closer. I broke into a dash. I made the door and was out. Cool outside air fell into me. I turned and walked slowly and coolly past the front window in case anyone left in the downstairs office might be looking out. I could see the corner. *The others must be well gone by this stage.* I heard the door bang shut behind me. *They're outside too don't turn around.* I walked briskly. I kept my head down. My car was there in front of me. I took my keys out with dishonest nonchalance. Thanked God that I had a buzzer. I was in and safe. I looked at my phone as my colleagues swarmed past me and into their cars. I hadn't said a word to my colleagues all day. *Maybe tomorrow.*

I drove and thought. The therapist was going to lead me on a journey through the things that were blocking my growth as a fully rounded person and professional. I was ready for this. I was sick of living from the neck up.

I arrived at the therapist's house. I waited until a little past my due time to make sure I did not bump into anyone else on the way out. I pictured a person in hysterics and embarrassed to be seen by another person. Maybe I pictured myself.

I sat down on a comfy chair facing the hypno-therapist. The room was very warm. I thought about removing my jacket to make myself

C1: Head

more comfortable. I calculated the movements necessary to achieve this, from standing up, stretching, sliding, turning, hanging, turning and sitting. I left my jacket where it was. An image flashed into my head, a second and then gone, *stuck, playground, wall, rotten bananas*. I had become adept at batting these images away.

'How was your day today?'

'Is there anything you'd like to talk about before we begin?'

'It's just the usual. I've barely spoken all day.'

'You're speaking fine now?'

'I know. I have permission to speak now'

'Ok. When you first came here you spoke about Selective Mutism. I don't like to put labels on things. I believe everything can be traced back to your belief system. I want you tell me about your experiences. I want you to relax, close your eyes and picture yourself as an explorer travelling from your head, down your spine and into a pool of tranquility in your pelvic basin. Imagine in this pool is the truth of you. Imagine unscrambling your way through the entwined dark growth of your past. Imagine the sun above reaching those neglected dark areas as they are cut back of their overgrowth. I want you to feel and let go. When you hear me clap you are to wake up'.

C2: Sick

Uuuuugh, Uuuuugh, Uuuuugh.

I concentrate on the white dotty hospital ceiling to take my mind away from my constricted breathing. I try to find familiar shapes in the dots to take me back to home and away from this place.

A rustling of the curtain draws my attention. A hand appears between the curtains and pulls them apart. A priest is standing at the side of my bed. He sits down. "Through this holy anointing may the Lord in his love and mercy help you with the grace of the Holy Spirit, May the Lord who frees you from sin save you and raise you up". *Yesterday I was fine.*

The curtains part again. My parents sit beside me. 'You're very sick with the croup. You're going to have to go to the children's hospital in Dublin. You'll be brought up in an ambulance'. Images of flashing lights and sirens and cars careering out of the way come into my head.

A nurse wheels me through the long white corridors of the hospital. I float past other wrecks, some walking slowly along the wall holding onto bars for support, others pushing themselves in wheel chairs, others stationary in stretchers with arms reaching up.

There is a clanging noise as we move over something. We enter into a small space and two doors slide shut. The nurse presses a button and we begin to move. I feel like I've left myself behind. We stop. The doors open. A wall of noise enters the small space. The nurse

C2: Sick

wheels me out over the clang again and out through a set of sliding doors. I am hit by the cold of the evening. She hands the stretcher over to two ambulance men. I hear a bang and then the doors are closed.

I am moving fast. I feel again like I've left myself behind. The siren sounds when-ever we slow down too much. I feel a tingle in my toe like I'm perched over the edge of a high place. There is a tube stuck down my throat, it makes breathing easier. I look up at the ceiling. I look around the ambulance. I see my Mum. 'It's ok, you'll be alright'. I feel a chill at the thought of the end of the trip and the beginning of something else. The blankets have become warm and I'm used to them. The ambulance comes to a stop. The back doors are flung open. It's cold again. Ambulance men pull the stretcher out with me wrapped in on top.

Doctors and nurses mill around. They put strange cold things on me and stick a needle into my arm. I fall asleep.

I awake in a bed. I look around at the strange environ I've been landed in. Everything is different to what I'm used to. There are strange smells and people in white gowns. I look down towards my feet. I am captured in a white blanket and sheet. Beside and opposite me are three other beds each with a surrounding curtain rail. Within each there is a sickly looking child in pajamas. Adorning the walls are colorful bold hand of child paintings. My parents are at the side of my bed. 'You're going to be okay. You gave us a bit of a fright'. I fall asleep again.

Persona Medusa

I awake. I look for my parents. They're not here. I want to call for them. I don't. I don't want to draw attention. If this alien place knew I was here it would eat me up. I lay sideways, front-ways, back-ways, any which ways wishing to be home.

A nurse takes me out of bed and shows me around. There's a play room with low tables and small chairs. On the tables are brightly colored toys, art materials and puzzles. I take in the sights and sounds of other children's play. The nurse brings me over to a spare place at one of the tables and leaves the room. I sit. I wonder how to get back to the safety of the bedroom that I know and away from this strange place within a strange place. I do not touch the toys. A television glares up high on a metal shelf in the corner of the room. I look at the TV. I cannot play here. The nurse arrives back and takes me by the hand back to my room. I climb back into my bed and wonder where my parents are. I know I'm a long way from home.

I begin to recognize the routine, breakfast at eight thirty, lunch at one, dinner at six, playroom after lunch.

Like the rising sun a small face appears over the edge of my bed. 'What's wrong with you?' I do not answer. The small boy reaches out his hand and starts tapping my arm for a response. I do not respond. As if to make a move or a sound would be to announce my presence and that I am ok with being here.

In the night as I lay awake strange sounds arrive into my ear. Some seem to come from far off from scary dimly lit rooms off long corridors. Others more suddenly, jumpily, a metal tray being dropped,

C2: Sick

a loud scream let go. A disinfectant smell permeates the air. Shadows of things I cannot identify pass my sight. I cannot move. To outstretch my hand into the beyond from under the covers would be to invite a creature from beneath to grab it and drag me under and devour me.

My parents are here. It is the weekend. I speak. I tell of all the things I did during the week. I leave out the toy room and the not speaking for the past week. They tell me it is time to go home.

I look out the rear window of the car. The hospital grows smaller as we move away. I turn my head and look forward between the car seats watching as we pass into and out of small towns and villages.

We arrive home, back to the comforts of my own bed, the heavy tucked in blankets, the familiar shapes with their familiar shadows and the familiar night time noises.

I lay in bed letting the memories from the past two weeks flood into my head. I see long white coats, disinfectant smells and colorful playrooms. I turn my head into the corner and pull the blankets up further. I imagine the blankets as a shield to keep everything out. I drift into sleep.

C3: Death

I am at my Grandparents house in the countryside.

The sun shines brightly in the blue sky. All is peaceful. A haze hovers above the dug up ground. I crunch around in my boots in the dry mud with my plastic red shovel. I try to dig furrows for planting potatoes. Frustration up-heaves me when the shovel bends instead of slicing the earth. I tilt my head to the side and see my Grandfather holding a metal spade with a wooden handle. I watch as he bends his knee, lifts his boot on to the shoulder of the spade, grimaces slightly, exerts downward pressure and meeting with lesser resistance, parts the earth. I look again at my red shovel. Again I attempt to dig but again it bends. I raise myself up. I catch a glimpse of a sudden movement. Sunlight glints like a transparent fan at the corner of my eye. I hear something, an expulsion of air, an attempted intake. My Grandfathers spade falls to the ground. A wisp of dust raises then drifts. I watch root stuck and punch struck. His white shirt flaps in the slight breeze. His hand rises to clutch his chest. His knees drop and hit the ground. He bends over. He forms a fist and beats down on the earth, twisting, leaning forward, gasping, hands opening and clutching. His head meets the ground. He stretches and gasps.

All the stories that he told flash in my mind. *Shuck! shuck! unleashing whip two big work horses driving forward dust rising dirty road pointy ears two towered Cathedral two big limestone blocks lying rope stayed lurching striking stone ground wishing journey end*

◀ C3: Death

two more visiting night knocking neighbors door sitting down cup of tea chatting cows potatoes walking down road water pump cold wash outside sitting dark splotched wall cap head warm.

I look up. The blue sky above is scattered with changing racing clouds. Birds chatter and sing in rustling leafy sun full trees all around.

I drop my shovel. I inch a few steps closer to the man mound on the ground, a game maybe, but there's something too still. I feel like there's tickling ivy growing and climbing up my body from my toe to my head. I turn and run. The air presses against and passes my body. I reach the back door of the house and push it open. 'Why has Grand-dad gone to sleep in the muck?' I ask calmly and cute like, though I know it is too still for sleep. An image of dirt on white shirt fills my mind. He was always immaculate. My Dad shoots a look out the window. He leaps from his seat. 'Phone an ambulance!' He rushes past my shoulder. I see him through the window running over the dried open earth kicking loose clay in his wake. My Mam picks up the phone and turns the dial. I rush out the door to follow my Dad.

Everything seems still and hushed despite the forward racing. A crow still and quiet high on the black slunk electric wire cable over-looks the scene. I trip in one of the furrows. My horizon falls. I see more earth than sky. I raise and brush myself off. I see my Dad reach the stillness on the ground and kneel down beside him. He clasps his hands together and begins to apply pressure onto his chest. Inside my own chest my heart thumps rapidly. He pinches his nose and blows into his mouth. He thumps his heart, again and again, frantic. I hear the screaming of a siren coming from far off. It gets closer and louder.

The ambulance appears flashing and wailing over the dark splotchy cracked mossy garden wall. The siren stops, silence. The lights still light and turn. The door opens and a man jumps out. He lays a hand on the wall and leaps over with his medical bag. He kneels down beside my Grandfather on the ground and begins to try and revive him. The high perched crow on the wire shoots into the air with a loud flapping burst. They pick him up and put him on a stretcher and place him into the ambulance. I watch as the ambulance speeds away up the road and over the hill out of view. I drop my eyes and follow the white road marking back to my toes. I stand still with hung head. I follow the others back to the house.

The adults gather together smoking and talking. I stand in front of the black wooden gate leading to the muck of the farmyard. A few chickens claw, scrapple, scratch, peck, cluck and jerk around. A turkey appears gobbling behind them. Beyond in the field a cow bellows. In the teeming trees the birds chirp and sing. I hear the crunch of the gravel beneath my feet. I don't want to turn around.

The phone rings. He is dead.

◼ C4: New Territory

My Dad and I approach the prefab hut which houses the junior infant's school. It lies there in front of me like a crocodile's snout. I can see the teacher through the blinded window. She is standing in the middle of the room. She mustn't see us approaching. I hope she never sees me. With each step closer I take I feel like a tonne weight is being slowly pushed to the back curve of my tongue, disappears over and drops into the dark of my throat where it stays in perpetual fall.

We reach the front door and head into the entrance hall way. My Dad wraps on the classroom door with his finger knuckles. *Why did he have to do that? We were safe out here unseen, unheard.* It sounds like there is a herd of elephants trumpeting and stampeding inside. The entire hut shakes as if buffeted by bulbous nose hippos. 'Schhhhhh'. *Who said that?* My legs are heavy and stiff. They know I'm here, late. *Why could I not have been early now I'll stick out like a sprung duck.* I shiver though I feel the warmth of the sun against my bare legs. A red crisp packet whisks past the open front door. *I wish I could move free and away like that.* I feel a gentle breeze cause the tiny hairs on my leg to move. I imagine them as thousands of long reeds by a riverside rustling and drawing attention. *Why did I not wear long trousers to hide such movements?* I stiffly move my head and look up at my Dad. He lays his huge hand on top of my head and mashes my hair. It doesn't make me feel any better. I hear footsteps coming towards the door. A geyser shoots ice cold water up my spine turning my brain into a roiling stormy thundery sky. The footsteps come to a halt. A woman's voice comes from the other side of the door. 'Quiet! Please!' I look up at my Dad. His hand is on my shoulder. I feel its weight. He whispers to me. 'The first day is always the hardest'.

I watch as the door handle descends to a guillotine slope. It pauses there. I feel like a cold blade has sliced through me. I focus on a thin sliver of light at the edge of the door. It begins to widen like a sunlit knife slowly turning sideways.

A teacher steps into the guillotine rectangle. At first my eyes focus on her. She talks over my head to my Dad. The sound of moving stretching chairs and desks attracts my attention. I look around her legs and see eyes shooting in my direction from behind desks. The smells, the sounds, the sights whoosh forward into me. My ribs clasp tight around me like a predators claw. I wind my gaze back to my current location. I feel like I have just caught and eaten a big wet cold flapping fish which now lies at the pit of my stomach. I wish I had a bucket to hand like the one I had that night when I was sweating and throwing up at the side of my bed. That was so handy. I don't know where anything is here.

The teacher glances back at the class and commands, 'Quiet'. She pulls the door shut. The class murmurs behind her and the door. Her eyes rise to heaven and a smile stretches her mouth. A smile to me would normally be warm and inviting but this strikes me as a limp trap waiting to spring up and catch me.

C4: New Territory

She reaches out her hand and shakes my Dads hand. She slowly lowers herself to my level and looks me in the eyes. 'Hi DJ Welcome to school'. I try to say 'Hi' back but it feels like I'm pulling an electrical barbed wire up my throat. I look up at my Dad and then back at the teacher and nod. All warmth has gone from me. I don't shiver, that would be seen and I would be seen. The teacher reaches out and places a white sticker on my shirt with my name written in bold black. I feel the pressure of her finger as she applies the sticker. I hope she can't feel what I feel through her finger, through my shirt. I would be exposed. *Nobody can know maybe I could transfer my feelings to her maybe the last person to have touched the person with this feeling will have it like a game I could play at home.*

My mind darts back to this time yesterday when I was running around in the cull de sac outside my house playing Catch and shouting 'you're it' whenever I was on and touched someone. I did not feel like this then.

The teacher rises, runs hers hands over her skirt, she looks at my Dad. 'I'll take him in'. She stands aside and stretches out her open hand. 'Come in DJ. I'll show you to your desk'. She points to a desk at the back of the class on which sits a paper prism with my name on it. The letters are bigger and bolder than I have seen before.

The teacher's fingers close around my hand. I feel a force pulling me. My feet become unstuck and I begin moving forwards towards the rectangle of the door. I allow it to happen, as if somehow I think it is unreal, that this is a nightmare and I will wake up before the terrible thing happens. I get closer and closer to the door. I get tenser and tenser. The closer I get the more I realize that this is real. The Teacher passes through the door and into oblivion eyes. I step into the framed space of the door frame.

The rush of the new bombards me. I scan the class room space. The blue hairy fuzzy floor is overlooked by a white dotty ceiling like a stormy sky over a dagger sea. Smiles curl like scythes on wonder fallen faces. A toy bright yellow digger bares its shovel teeth. Plasticine shapes lay stretched and deformed like chewed and spat out limbs. Desks with black metal legs bide their time. Whispers hiss in the air. Spearhead eyes from within dark caves point towards me. On the wall blood streaked pictures hang. Plastic blue chairs peck and squeak. At the front the unblinking shark eye blackboard watches over everything. The air is heavy with strange new smells, paint, plasticine, disinfectant, crayons, so dense and heavy that I could eat the smells themselves if I could open my mouth.

A bell hammer goes off in the middle of my brain. A fountain of icy cold water shoots up my spine and makes an icy cold sponge spool of my brain. My hair turns into sharp needles and prods inwards. Harpoons tear through my elbows. My head turns right then left then right, then left over and over. My hands spring out and grab hold of the door frame. Tears emerge and slide over my cheeks and into my eyes. Everything becomes blurry. 'Don't be scared. Go on in. They won't bite you'. I try to reverse out of the door frame but come up against a flat obstruction. I dare not turn. I feel the teachers open

C4: New Territory

psalm against my back. I lose my balance and fall forwards. The world before my eyes curves as my head bows to look at the ground. My right foot shoots forward to re-gain my balance. A dart strikes me under sole. My foot shoots back. My grip tightens on the door frame. My Dad grabs my hand on one side and the Teacher on the other. They try to prise my hands open one finger at a time. They wrap their arms around mine and try to pull me away from the door. With every force I feel I respond with a life or death strength in the opposite direction. An unending avalanche falls in my white blinded mind.

They stand back. The teacher in front of me. My Dad behind. A red lolly pop is produced and is waved in front of my eyes. The red lolly pop enters my head like a burning swirling circular saw. My head shakes furiously. My lips seal.

The teacher gestures to my Dad to wait a minute then turns and walks over to one of her new junior infant students. The class averts its eyes from the doorway to follow the teacher's movements. The threats acting upon me abate. I stare forward through the white of my mind, my tear washed eyes and into the class space.

The teacher returns. Beside her is a student. 'He wants to be your friend'. My body tenses. *This can't be true.* My hands grip tighter. My mind whitens whiter. My head shakes. The student reaches out his hand. 'Come on in, you can sit beside me'. Multiple dilated pupil eyes train back on me, on us, the disturbance in the door frame. I cannot budge. Certain death is in there.

Persona Medusa

The teacher puts her hands on her hips. She ushers me back out of the frame and into the hallway and closes the door. Their arrow eyes can't penetrate to here. My Dad kneels down to my level. 'Take your time'.

I take my time in the hope that we can go home. An image has formed in my head of me standing in the door frame like a painting in a gallery that everyone can gather around and look at. I cannot allow that to happen again. It accomplished the opposite of my need not to be seen. 'Are you ready?' I nod my head.

My Dad opens the door. I see the door frame. I will not be grabbing hold of that this time. I stand at the top of the class. I see the desk with the paper prism and my name. It seems a million miles away through a storm of eyes. The teachers hand appears over my head. She's beckoning for someone to come up. I see the same student loosen himself from his grey plastic seat and come forward. He stands in front of me. 'We can be friends'. I'm moving. All eyes follow us.

I sit down on a seat at the back of the class room. The grey plastic closes in on me. I feel like there is a cold stone resting in my middle. I sit still.

C5: Stepping on a Twig

My sit beside neighbor turns around. He places one arm on the back of my seat and the other on my desk. 'What's your name?' He knows my name. It is written on the desk in front of me. It doesn't matter. I want to respond but I can't. All I see is one figure in a firing squad that's going to get bigger. My middle turns into an icy whirlpool. My throat shrinks. I want to speak. I want to say my name. Each time I think to speak I am crushed. Fiercer and fiercer each time. It is as each potential sound making breath is a vial of poison that if broke and released will kill me. I breathe silently. I try to defeat this feeling but I can't. My neighbor looks on with a puzzled look. 'What's your name?' Again my answer is silence. I stare into the distance as if I can see a herd of stampeding elephants appearing over the horizon. I dare not think. Thinking is like a hook for the feeling. The feeling is like a cold snake in a basket rising to the tune of speech and expectation. There is an anchor on my voice dropped down to a frozen ice pool in my pelvis. It is embedded there. It spreads freezing cold throughout my body whenever I try to loosen it. I think my thoughts are causing this feeling so I remove my mind from the situation altogether. 'Can you not speak?' This goes in like a knife. My response is silence. 'Is there something wrong with you?' The knife twists. I see other faces turn. 'He doesn't speak'. 'Leave him alone'. I don't want to be left alone but I don't want to be engaged either. There's too much space out there for my voice to be.

Persona Medusa

The teacher drops her shoulders and turns around from the blackboard. 'Silence Please'. My interrogators turn and face the front of the class. I am glad. 'We're only trying to get DJ to speak Ms'. She looks down at me. I am the center of attention again. A grain at the bottom of a shit chute. 'He'll speak when he's ready, isn't that right DJ?'

I feel a tickling in my nose. It's a familiar sensation. A sneeze is on its way. This at home would be an enjoyable experience. I would sneeze loudly and animatedly. I would enjoy the sensation of it being out of my control. I would let it happen. Let it go.

In this classroom the deep down feelings of muscular contraction are like two rods stuck into my head and an electrical charge passing through my brain. I cannot let this happen. I cannot be completely silent and then suddenly make this gigantic outburst. I imagine the turned heads and the stares and the 'I thought he couldn't speak'. I can feel the deep inside muscles begin to contract and air being drawn in. I need to do something quick before I make a sound. I think about raising my hand to my nose. I know if I pinch my nose I might be able to stop it. I imagine raising my hand but people will see. I sit still. My head goes backward and forward. *Did anyone see that?* It is out of my control. The sneeze is only a couple of seconds away. I look quickly forward and though my peripheral vision and make the decision to quickly lift my hand up and pinch my nose. The convulsions of expulsion occur but I hold it in and will it not to come out. It abates and I drop my hand quickly again as if nothing had happened. I have man-

C5: Stepping on a Twig

aged not to make any sound. I scan the classroom. Nobody seems to have noticed.

I am learning how to write by using a pencil and making letters on a wide lined page. My nib is getting shorter. I have a pencil sharpener with me in my pencil case. I imagine what's involved in getting the sharpener and sharpening the pencil. I would have to pick up the pencil case. Pull back the zipper. Rustle around inside to find the sharpener. Take out the sharpener. Turn the pencil around and around until it comes out sharp. Discard of the left over bits. I look to see if anyone else is sharpening their pencils. Nobody is. I decide to slow down my writing until the end of the class and sharpen my pencil when I get home. *I will get a pencil sharpener with an attached bin that will collect the shavings that will solve one problem are they expensive though.* There is a larger mechanical pencil sharpener on the teacher's desk which everyone else uses and I really want to use. I imagine pulling back my chair. Sliding out of the chair. The squeak. Standing up straight. Walking between the other desks. The expectation to say sorry if I bang into another desk. Walking from behind people to out in front of them and into their gaze. Standing beside the teacher's desk. Putting my pencil into the machine. Turning the knob. Hoping that it works. The expectation to speak if it doesn't work. The whirring sound the machine will make. And then the walk back. I remain where I am. I go back to my writing and watch the nib of my pencil as it is slowly eaten away.

Persona Medusa

The teacher announces play time. I see two white long toy shelves running the perimeter of the room. There are diggers, cars, jigsaws, dolls and other funny looking things all stacked up there. I want to play with these toys. The other children are rushing forward to pick up a toy. I remain stationary. I make a plan to pretend that I've already been up and have got a toy. The other children argue over certain fanciful toys, move around, glance bodies, shriek, and eventually return to their respective desks with toys in hand. I move my psalms up on the desk so the teacher or anyone else might think that I have a toy behind them. I have no problem getting and playing with toys at home.

C6: Tiger Eyes

I look up towards the front of the class. On the Teachers desk sits a large book, grey with black cornered edges. She opens the book and wielding a red pen in one hand and a ruler in the other bows her head to its outstretched contents. I see her eyes hovering above the book between the pencil holder and stapler and piles of copy books. 'Quiet, for the roll call, please'.

The cold stone in my middle expands. She calls out a name. 'Here'. Her finger moves down the page. She calls out another. 'Here'. It dawns on me that the names are being called out in alphabetical order. I do the math in my mind. It's the surnames. My name will be close to the end. My breath feels like freezing fog. I breathe faster. The cold stone in my middle drops to my bottom. It freezes everything in its path. It pulls everything down to its cold center. *Does anyone notice?* I do not want anyone to notice. I do not want to be different to everyone else. Her hand makes a stroke after each name she calls. *Does anyone else feel like I do?* She swings her head up after each utterance, listens, looks and locks, recognizes and bows her head again. I sit ice block still. The cold stone expands and takes over my body. I dare not shiver.

With each name called the colder I get. 'DJ'. She looks up. She calls my name again. 'DJ'. She sees me. She knows who I am. She knows I'm here. 'DJ'. The cold stone is drawing everything down. I do not even think that I should speak. The thought and freeze come so soon together that they are one and the same. The boy beside me comes to my rescue 'He's here, Ms'. She moves her red pen up and down like a tiger ripping at my intestines after the kill. My name is ticked off. The cold stone explodes and reforms.

I can think again. *What just happened? Will it happen again?* I sit cold. I don't make a sound. Even of breathing. *If I do make a sound then they will know I can make a sound then they will wonder why I don't make a sound then they will think he's afraid to make a sound then they'll think he's weak not to make a sound.*

The teacher speaks from the top of the classroom. Children raise their hands and ask questions. They speak and whisper and laugh. I am in awe at their ability to do this. I do not speak or make noise of any sort. I look straight ahead into the shark eye blackboard behind her.

◆ C7: Camouflage

I avoid the thought of speaking or moving. I look at the clock. I hear a bell ringing in the distance. I see the teacher stand up and the other boys and girls shuffling in their seats. 'Stand Up'.

Within and covered by the noise of standing bodies and pushed back seats I stand up. 'Line up in twos in front of the door'. I walk slowly wondering who I'll stand beside. I join the line at the back. I stare at the back of the persons head in front of me. Another child is forced to stand beside me.

Teacher leads us out the door and towards a small black metal gate in a low dark splotched concrete wall. Through the bars in the gate I can see children flitting past and I can hear shouts and screams.

My mind future flings through the gate and into the yard. The thought of screaming and moving causes the cold stone to expand and shrink in my middle.

I continue moving now as part of a whole. *If I can stick with my class I won't look out of place.* Teacher pulls back the latch on the gate and pushes it open. 'It's play time children, enjoy yourselves'.

The heads in front of me rush forward under the teachers arm and through the gates screaming. They disperse in all directions. I walk through the gate. My feet feel heavy. They're trying to pull me backwards. My cover is gone. The whole is now just I.

Persona Medusa

I look for a safe place, somewhere where no-one might see me, where I wouldn't look out of place or seem to be hiding, a place in the middle of everything but separate from everything. I look to the wall.

I move backwardly forwards toward the wall. I try to outwardly look unaffected. My feet stick. I feel like I'm walking on sharp nails. I can make out details of the wall as I get closer. It is black and splotchy. I'll be safe there when I can blend into its darkness. *How will I turn around?* I reach the wall. I turn around expecting something terrible to be there. There are children playing.

My body feels heavy. My bones are made of lead. I stand statue still and stare across the playground. It is a tarmac area bounded by four low dark walls and a small metal gate. White lines mark out snakes and ladders and hop-scotch. I would have liked to have had a look around here before entering. I can feel the walls rough solidity against my back and my psalms. At my feet orange peels, banana skins, discarded crusts of sandwiches and crushed milk cartons lay strewn. I can taste their smell. I have a lunch box but I can't move to open it. *What will I tell my parents when I bring my lunch home?*

I know I should move. Everyone else is moving. I'm stuck on the thought action tip of an arrow strike. I can see what's in front of me and what's beside me. The wall has my back. Everyone I see, boys, girls, teacher, are all sharp toothed predators, waiting for movement to highlight my existence to them and then I between their teeth.

♦ C7: Camouflage

My fingers bend and claw upwards and downwards over the rough surface. I see these movements as being done out of sight between the shadow of my leg and the wall. I wish the black tar would absorb me. I wish I could move further backwards and merge into the wall. Nobody could see me then. I would have to do it though when no one is watching. There I could think rational thoughts.

To my left and right there are timber benches. I know that if I sit down there I would be less conspicuous. This thought is easy. The actions required to achieve this flash on my mind, from stuck fixed position, to turning sideways, walking forward, turning around front ways, bending my knees, buttocks touching the seat and straightening my back. There is a flood of thoughts that don't involve action by me but do act to give reason to the already aborted attempt. *That person over there looks like he could be heading over to take that seat if I start to move towards there and then have to turn back then everybody will see and I will look foolish and then what if my previous spot is taken I would have to venture into the open space where free play is happening No I would be seen by everyone they would know I am not comfortable I haven't moved in ages if I move now it would look unusual.*

An uncomfortable lurching feeling radiates upwards from my stomach. A vision forms in my mind of getting sick. I had been sick lots of times before. I know it's messy. I now see myself wrapping my arms around my stomach as convulsions radiate upwards forcing me to bend in two and letting everything empty heavily, striking and scattering, onto the black tarmac surface. Maybe some would scatter on some ones shoe. An apology would be expected. I would be expected to speak. *No, No, No.* This could not happen. 'Listen everyone, he can speak'. People would turn and look. My prey image would pass through eyes and into predator brains. I will my stomach to settle.

An image forms of me stepping away from the wall and into open space. I cannot imagine myself approaching people or people approaching me. This is alien to me. Everyone and everything seem to be far horizons that I can never reach. I cannot step into that empty space to try and bridge the distance.

Children screaming and chasing each other come closer then move away. I hear their games. 'Ring a ring a Rosie, pocket full of posies, a tissue, a tissue, we all fall down'. They hold hands and spin in a circle and fall down laughing. 'Tag, you're it'. They chase each other screaming. I want to play. It is impossible.

Children stand at the wall beside me in groups excitedly chatting to each other. These distract other searching predator eyes from me. The be-side me group becomes a shadow sanctuary to me. Then they move. I am never privy to their plans to move in unison into the out there space. I watch as they depart. The arrow eyes of those out there fly towards me.

I think to myself. *I look like a fool standing here I must move I will go closer to the group beside me.* I inch sideways along the wall like a slow boat hugging the shore until I am in close proximity to the nearest group. I stand close to them and push myself from the wall.

◆ C7: Camouflage

I'm just at the wall cause I'm so laid back if the wall wasn't behind me I'd fall over. I try to listen to what is being said. I look over shoulders. I think of something to say. The thought comes to me like a hole in a boat. I am sunk down and engulfed in a whirlpool. No sound comes. No laugh. I stand silently. The group moves. I follow pretending to belong. I am noticed. 'What are you doing here, have you no friends of your own'. I stand transfixed and unable to answer. The group moves away. I stay stuck. I backtrack back to the wall.

A boy from out there is moving towards me. He's got a smile on his face. He's like a slow moving torpedo moving through a substance that everyone else is connected to and that I cannot grasp. I do not move my eyes. I know what happens when I think of speaking or of movement. He stands beside me panting, sweating, full of after fun life. 'What's the matter?' 'Why don't you play?' I cannot answer. I want to answer. The thought to speak is akin to jumping into a fast moving river knowing that I will be carried swiftly away and drown. I dare not dip my toe. I do not make any movement. I see myself as being observed by others like I'm at the bottom of a magnifying glass. 'Can you not speak?' My answer is silence. He reaches out his arms and grabs me by the wrists. He starts to pull me away from the wall into the out there space. He's using his weight to shift me from my stationary position. My spine turns to ice. I picture myself as the bottom of a whirlpool with the swirls of peoples' attention bearing in on me. I pull backwards. I resist every movement. In my peripheral vision I can see heads turning, the wall moving, what's beyond the wall

Persona Medusa

moving, the ground moving. I am moving. I continue staring straight ahead. My head begins to shake, involuntarily. I do not speak. 'Come on out'. I am away from the wall, in the out-there. He lets go of me. He stands back and laughs. Others look perplexed. I feel like I'm falling with nothing to reach out and hang onto, like that nightmare that I wake up from. I turn and walk back to the safe solidity of the wall.

I watch from my wall framed safe place as he moves away and into the throng of activity. He approaches a group of boys and joins in the play and speech. This is amazing to me. It is like Jesus walking on water.

A teacher strides across the yard. She holds a bell in her hand. *Does she see me like this I hope not I don't want her to know that I'm out of the ordinary here.* She circles the playground. She rushes over to where a scuffle has broken out and breaks it up. She passes close by me, stuck to the wall me. *Not the real me.* I am buffeted by the air as she strides past. *Does she notice that everyone else is talking playing but I am not I hope she does not I can pretend there's nothing wrong.*

I see her arm rise like a canon pointed at me. Two children stand be-side her looking up and listening to what she is saying. They break away and head in my direction. I know she has spotted me and has dispatched these two children to try and play with me. I hope I am imagining it. They stand beside me. 'Do you want to play?' I look over their shoulders as they surround me. I see the teacher standing still like the last remaining domino amidst the fallen of my imaginary

C7: Camouflage

guards. I can't reply. 'There's nothing to be scared of, come on', I know they're right but still I can't. They look back at the teacher and shake their heads. She moves off. They move off. My imaginary guards spring up again.

I feel the solidness of the wall behind my back. No eyes can pierce it. I can see everyone in front. I look forward to when the bell rings to end this play time and I can go back to my seat. I don't know where to be here and I can't go anywhere.

She raises her large bell and drops it, and again and again, break is over. The teachers enter the playground and stand along a line. Everyone runs over to their respective teacher's line. There is still some shouting and screaming in the top right corner of the playground which seems darker to me than the rest. It seems the furthest place in the world to me. Maybe if the playground was empty of children I would venture up there but for now I am at the wall. I have somewhere to go now. I leave the wall. I hear screaming and footsteps from all around. *What's happening behind me?* The Teacher is organizing us into a straight line in twos. I approach the line as slowly as I can get away with.

Now I can move.

I go back to my desk. The teacher announces the school tour. It is a trip to Dublin Zoo. Everyone is excited. I feel like the teacher has just flung a spear at me from the top of the class and I am now impaled upon it. I do not stir. She hands out permission slips to be signed by parents. I see the slip as my own death warrant that I have to sign. I begin to conjure excuses to get out of it. It is hard though to say I can't go when everyone else is so excited and happy about going. People will think me strange if I act differently to everyone else. I bring the slip home. My Mam signs it. I hand it back I like a slow motion scene in a horror movie. That's it for me.

I wonder dazed like I've just exited a bomb blitz. I walk around the apple tree at home. I look at the apples small still *they can remain in the same place and grow why do I have to move and speak to people.* I am full of sugar. The world is a blur.

At last the day arrives. I am crippled over. I just want this over with so I can carry on with my life and look forward to the summer holidays. The bus arrives and we all board. I find a seat close to the top but neither the middle or the top. I sit clutching my lunch bag. *How where am I going to eat this* I can smell it and just want it gone. I look out the window and watch the green patchwork landscape pass by. It is warm in here. I wish the journey would never end. The others shout and sing. I smile but my face muscles hurt.

We are here. We are led around by teacher to gaze upon the animals. Each child stares in wonder at each enclosure. The animals are the attention receivers. I just have to follow the group and look at these animals. This is easy. The thing that scares me is the upcoming playground time and the picnic time.

We enter the playground. It is a sand covered log fenced enclosure. There are slides, swings, see-saws and merry go-rounds. My class-mates run for these things.

♦ C7: Camouflage

I inch my way towards the slide. I make it to the base of the ladder and look up. I have turned to stone. 'Weeeee What are you standing there for Weeeee come on up hello Weeeee'. Children flit past me on their way from their slide to the ladder to slide again. I cannot even move to get away from this situation. I am the submarine and they are the fish.

The teacher calls out 'Playtime over, everyone form a line, in twos, please'. I follow the others towards the teacher.

'It's picnic time' the teacher says. We enter a green area. There are timber seats around but we sit on the ground. I remain standing until everyone else is seated in their groups. I reach the ground after a slow descent. There is only me in my group. I hope the teacher doesn't notice. I open my bag and eat my lunch. I have managed to sit and eat my lunch and I am happy with this.

◆ T1: Shedding Coat

It is cold. My breath forms a mist in front of my face. All of us school children are lined up to enter the class room. Everyone I see has a coat on. I knew they would, there is no reason for them not to. I left my coat behind me this morning on purpose.

'Have you no coat? You look freezing?' I shake my head. My interrogator looks perplexed at me. *I don't need a coat I'm hard like that.*

There is laughter behind me. 'You stand beside him'. A boy is pushed in beside me. 'Why do you not speak?' I cannot answer. More children line up behind us. They are laughing and talking. The be-side me boy turns his head over his shoulder and joins in the fun. My skeleton is lead and my blood is ice.

The line starts to move and I follow with it. I notice my shoe lace is undone but I can't do anything about it. I try my best not to trip. I would be expected to give out in some fashion or maybe say sorry to somebody. To step out of line and bend down and ty it is completely unthinkable. Thinking is unthinkable. There is less expectation to speak when moving. A part of the energy required for speech must go into making the legs move. I can see the class room and I look forward to my seat. Hopefully I will not have to move again.

We all walk through the door. I see the desks, four two seat desks lined up touching each other with no gaps, eight people in a line. My seat is fourth one in.

◆ **T1**: Shedding Coat

Everyone has coats to hang-up. I don't. This is my plan. I walk past the huddle at the coat hangers. I am first to arrive at my desk stretch. *My plan has worked.* I will escape the embarrassment of being unable to ask the first or second sitter to move so I can get by.

I slide into my seat, feigning effortlessness. *Nobody suspects a thing.*

◆ T2: Twit Twoo

The teacher stands in front of the shark's eye blackboard with a long ruler in her hand surrounded by white chalk letters like teeth. Her eyes are fixed on me. *She knows.* She points her ruler at me and takes aim along its length. 'You, what is your name?' I don't know much but I do know my name but I cannot answer. She strides over to my desk and looms over me. She bangs her ruler down in front of me with a loud scaring slamming noise that ruffles and rifles the class. Other on-looking heads snap back to the front. 'I asked you a question!' I cannot answer. She bangs her ruler again. 'Answer me!' 'He doesn't speak'. A girl has come to my rescue. The teacher leans across my desk and looks straight into my eyes. 'He doesn't speak, that's ridiculous, we'll soon see about that' 'What is your name?' 'What is your age?' 'Where are you from?' 'Why do you not speak?' I cannot answer.

She stops asking me questions and rises up and away from me. I hope that this is the end of the inquisition and she will move onto someone else. Her hand reaches out, grabs me by the collar and drags me up to the front of the class. I can feel the class looking at me. This is out of my control. She grabs my hand and pulls it towards her. She opens my fist so the fingers lay out straight, suspended in the mid air. She reaches backwards with her ruler. *Is she going to hit me on the fingers or the psalm why hadn't I noticed this before?*

◆T2: Twit Twoo

I remember other children when they were being lined up for a smack of the ruler that they'd rub their hands together furiously, this would cause small black bits of dead skin to form on their hands. These bits would absorb the stinging pain of the smack. I try to lift my hands, place them together and rub them but the thought to do this causes a freezing geyser to erupt inside. *It's too late for me now anyways.*

She brings the ruler swishing down with a loud slap on my fingers. This shocks me. *I thought it would be the psalm.* She does the same with the other hand. 'Speak!'

The pain is not as bad as the sound it makes. It's more numbing than anything. It is the slap sound that is causing tears to well up behind my eyes. This teacher is making sound out of me. She is causing me to be noticed. I must not show tears as well.

'Back to your seat' I turn away from her. My hands are beginning to sting more now. I feel my hands red warm. I feel like a million tiny needles are working their way up through my fingers. The tear welling gets stronger. No. *Is it worse because I didn't rub my hands together to form the black bits?*

◆ T3: Clearing

It is spring in the clearing.

I awake in the morning to a golden light coming in through the lightly curtained windows of my bedroom. The light draws me out from the warmth of my bed. I walk over to the window and draw back the curtains. The familiar scene of the cull de sac greets me, still early-empty. I rush down the stairs and devour my breakfast. I open the front door and the light floods in. There is still a chill in the air.

Across the road other children are appearing into the open. I pick up my bike and do an arc around the cul de sac, 'Hi Stephen, Hi Ruth, Hi Susan, Hi John' I say. I race up the road feeling the breeze press against me and the sun warm me. It doesn't take long before alongside me appear, Stephen and John. 'A race' I shout. We race up to the top of the road and back down again. We all shout and scream along the way. 'I win' screams Stephen. He's right.

I drop my bike and run over to Ruth and Susan who are sitting on the low red brick wall like two castle turrets, 'Do you want to come over to my house and play', I ask. They both jump off the wall, 'All right'.

We run shouting and screaming around the garden. We play. We sit and chat. We roll and loll around.

My Mum, Mary calls me in for lunch. I sit at the table. I laugh and eat and rush to get back out. I hear screams from outside and I am missing out.

T3: Clearing

I rush back out. We climb the hill leading up to the railway tracks. We're not allowed near the tracks so we play on the slope. We run down, catch onto slim trees and swivel around. We watch other people pass along the path below us.

I see my Dad, Tom comes in from work. I race down to greet him home.

We sit around the table for dinner. I ask for the butter. I ask for more potatoes. I laugh and talk. I play around the house with my toys. We sit and watch the black and white TV. I am warm and comfortable.

Night comes and I go to bed. I kneel at the side of my bed and whisper my usual night time prayer, 'God our father I come to say……'

It is summer in the clearing.

We have moved to the country side to my Grandparents house. I wake to a bright blue light coming in through the window. I pull back the curtains to an immense of sense, wood pigeon calling, birds singing, cows bellowing, chickens clucking.

I eat breakfast and rush out of the house and up the field at the back. I crawl through a gap in the hedge and meet up with John from the house over the field. He is the same age as me and goes to a different school. We walk and talk. I pick up a stick and swipe at nettles.

Together we meet up with other kids from the neighborhood. Andy, Jimmy and Mark. We head over the fields to the forest to play.

Persona Medusa

We talk, shout and shove. We moo at cows and beeeh at sheep along the way.

We enter the dark cool of the forest. Entwined trees block out all but twinkling light. Here we play at war. Two teams, unlimited sticks and base camps. I run, throw, hide and shout, all within the mighty forest.

I climb trees. Hang off branches casually. Swing from tree to tree, Tarzan like. I even mouth Tarzan's roar while thumping my chest. It's the most natural thing in the world to do. I run through leafy passages. Smooth slick leaves with raindrops slowly sliding brush against my skin. The branches slice the sunlight up on its journey to the ground. The ground is a patchwork quilt of light.

A flung stick heads directly towards me. It strikes me. I let out an expletive and rub my unfortunate self. I fling a stick at a head that appears from behind a fallen tree. It hits its target. Andy immediately drapes his hand around to the back of his head. His hand is covered in blood. 'Who threw that stick?' Nobody owns up. I decide not to get into trouble. *Keep quiet.* I feel powerful in my decision. This is me choosing to keep quiet. Andy walks home holding his head and has to go to hospital for stitches.

There is work to be done. The cows must have a store of food for the coming winter. Beneath a sky of utmost blue and afoot a field of harvest fabulous yellow we collect the hay which has been baled by machine. I clutch a bale, hoist it up onto my chest and then heave it up onto the trailer where it's grabbed again and stacked. Mary brings tea.

● T3: Clearing

'No fizzy drinks, there full of sugar, they'll make you more thirsty', the wise granny Caitlin says. The sun scorches down.

In the field beside us, the cows roam, rip the grass with their flat teethed mouths and swallow it to be kept for later digestion. Others look on chewing the cud, mouths moving, teeth grinding, big eyes watching. My mind shoots back to one of my lessons in school. *It regurgitates its food and chews the cud all day it's kind of like DJ there don't you're not in school now don't think about those things.*

The bales of hay are stacked high on the trailer. I sit on top, King of Hay. A length of straw hangs from my mouth. I suck and bite on it and let it casually hang there. The trailer bounces over the field. The burning fuel causes a black smoke to throw up into the blue sky. I lie down on the top bales and gaze at the blue of the sky.

'Hup'. The unloading begins. I grab a bale by the blue baling twine, hoist it up and lower it down to the man on the ground. He brings it into the shed and stacks it there. As evening falls and we feel the coolness of the air on our skin, the work ends, and we go inside for tea.

I go to bed and pray, '….thank you for your love today…..'

● T4: Foraging

A large rectangular board is brought into the classroom. Its surface is covered in colorful splashes of paint. It is laid on top of the desks in the middle of the room. All of us gather around. It is too wide on any side to reach across to the other. There is excitement in the air. I stand at the edge of the board. The teacher hands out blank white pieces of paper to each of us. There is a jar of brushes and a jar of paint within reaching distance. I pick up a brush and dip it in the jar of paint. I stroke the brush along the paper. I paint a stick man, ground and sun, tree and house. I paint them all in blue.

There is another color further away that I want to use but I cannot reach it. It would look stupid for me to walk around the perimeter of the table to get the jar. Any normal person would ask the person closest to the jar to pass it to them. I know I need to speak. I must ask. The thought to speak causes an upsurge of cold from the bottom of my spine to the top of my head. *Speak, speak do it now.* The feeling intensifies. I try to raise my hand to point at the jar. I think by doing this then words will follow. No. It is as if there is a puppet master controlling me with electric cables from beneath the floor that is pulling all my muscles down and electrocuting me at the same time. The harder I try to speak or to move the harder he pulls. I stop. I look at the jar on the far-side. It might as well be across the Atlantic Ocean.

I notice out of the corner of my eye a hand grab my blue jar. It's gone. I cannot continue with my painting. The pot of water is now out

T4: Foraging

of reach too. I move the already there blue color around. I try to look comfortable and at ease and not to be noticed. The brush gets dryer. The paint on the page gets dryer. I hold the brush over a blue part. I scan the page for a blotch maybe that didn't fully dry to reload. There is none. I flap my dry bristled brush on the paper. 'Do you need some paint?' My head moves up and down like it is impaled on a spear. 'All you had to do was ask'.

It is time for swimming lessons. My class and I traipse through the town in double file. I feign comfort. The person beside me turns his head to speak to the person behind or shouts forward to the person in front. *Speak, speak, speak.* It is accepted now that I do not speak, unusual as it is.

We enter the swimming pool complex and walk into the changing rooms. I reach out and grab a basket and place it down on the timber bench. I am wearing my swimming trunks underneath my clothes to save me the embarrassment of changing in front of others. I have to be organized like this. I undress and place my clothes in the basket, pick it up and walk to the poolside. I lay it down at the wall at the back of the swimming pool area and worry for a moment about what I'd do if someone stole my clothes.

Splashing, diving and cannon balling is what all the others do as I cling to the edge of the pool and wait for the structured learning to begin. I close my eyes and duck my head under water. I open my eyes. I can see other people from the chest down. It's funny watching them move without a head. Nobody can see me. I shake my head. I swish my arms through the water. For a few moments I am free. My breath is running out. I burst out of the water. I am flooded with relief of breath and life. There is too much noise and splashing for anyone to have noticed me. I contemplate doing it again but content myself with the memory being enough.

'Kick off from the wall. Arms out straight. The water is your friend'. The water comes into my mouth and I stop and stand up. I start again. I'm making noise in the water and moving too. It's like the water is my new camouflage. The wall I could never get into.

A loud horn blows for finish time. I pull myself from out of the pool. I grab my basket and head for the changing room. Droplets of water descend and race on my skin.

I put my basket on the bench and search in my bag for my towel. I push aside my clothes in the dark of my bag. There is something missing, jocks, socks, clothes but no towel. I feel like someone has just banged me on the back of my head with a brick. I have forgotten to pack my towel. *Of all the stupid things to do how did I forget my towel? Do I not know myself do I not know the awkwardness this is going to cause me?* I continue to search in my bag though I know it is not in there. *How did I let this happen I need to ask for a loan of a towel I need to let it be known that I'm in a situation say oh shit or something don't just stand here speak speak speak'.* I look around. Everyone else is busy drying themselves. I stand dripping with my hands rummaging in my bag still. The droplets still slide and descend. My fingers grasp around my school shirt. *I might be able to use that*

T4: Foraging

to dry myself pull it off just pat myself dry it kind of looks like a towel from a distance. I roll it up into a ball. I hope to everything that nobody notices. I casually pat dry the main areas of wet on my body. I dress myself over the remaining wet. I can feel the remaining wet penetrate my clothes. *I've gotten away with it.*

I sling my bag over my back and go to leave. The door is there. It seems to dissolve in a blur the closer I get. 'DJ, you're back is still wet'. I turn my head and look down my back. I'm kind of grateful and surprised to have been spoken too and for my name to have been used. 'Oh'. I shrug my shoulders. My voice sounds alien to me.

▪ T5: Open Defecation

I sit with the cold stone in my middle in the classroom. I feel my bowels begin to move. This is not a problem at home. In this class I have to raise my hand and ask for permission in Irish to go to the toilet. *An bhfuil cead agam dul go dti an leithreas.* This involves both movement and speech. This is impossible for me.

I feel my bowels move again. They groan. I consciously tighten my muscles. I swing my arm over my stomach to hide the groaning sound. I force myself rigid and lean forward. *Did anyone see that? Did anyone hear that?*

I have no choice but to try and hold it. There is only three hours left until home time. I try to act normal. I don't want it known that I need to go to the toilet or more accurately that I'm afraid to ask to go to the toilet. Just a pang now every twenty minutes. *I can hold it.*

I silently move my arms off the desk and drop them down to my sides. I clutch the sides of the plastic chair with both hands when the convulsions begin. My fingers are under the chair where no one can see them. *Hold it I must ask to go to the toilet come on just raise my hand please I can do it.* I am hit by an immediate rush, an inverted force of nature. The teacher seems a million miles away, through empty space. *How could I put my voice out into that immensity of a world it will be lost I'll be making shapes with my mouth and nothing will be heard so many heads in that space heads that would turn if I spoke.* Even the thought of speaking never mind the command to

■T5: Open Defecation

speak seems alien to me now. The convulsions stop. I feel like I'm floating over a meadow, all at peace. My fingers loosen their grip on the underside of my chair.

I imagine raising my hand to get the teachers attention and ask for permission. I imagine faces appearing where once were backs of heads, expecting me to speak, waiting for the words to come out. Each time I think of raising my hand it is followed by a rushing freezing cold spurt from bottom to top. Anytime I come close to raising my hand the rush quickens and intensifies. I cannot do it and to speak as well. My hand never makes it off the surface of the desk. *Someone might see me begin to initiate an action then expect me to follow through.* My arm feels like it's under the influence of an electric magnet under the ground. The more I will myself to do it the stronger the magnet gets. I feel like I am an anchor stuck deep in the earth. I tug on the chain but the more I tug the tighter the hold becomes. I cannot release myself out of myself to move or speak the necessary words. I sit and stare ahead as the turmoil happens inside. The powerful uncontrollable urges persist despite my best conscious efforts to ignore and put them down. I wish there was a second body around me and then I could work like these muscles I have no control over. They're powerful. The cold stone draws everything in, downwards, away from outward expression. I hold and hold and hold. *This doesn't happen to me at home.* I can't hold it for much longer. The convulsions are getting closer and closer and more intense. I imagine floating over calm meadows, of being free at home, of getting rid of a large weight and

Persona Medusa

floating free enjoying the sensation of weightlessness. Then the convulsions begin again. My knuckles go white with effort. The call of nature cannot be out-lasted. I give up the long struggle and let go in the classroom.

The dark clouds depart and I can see the sunshine for a brief spell. The smell permeates the room. People's heads turn.

The teacher assigns the job of cleaning me up to another boy. The toilets are situated in a different building. The boy takes me out to the toilets across the way. The breeze and the freedom as I step outside the prefab hut hit me as I walk laden down out. The magnet has followed me out of the classroom and is pulling everything down. My feet are heavy to lift.

The boy directs me into the toilets and into a cubicle. I cannot move. He hands me a roll of toilet paper. I cannot move. He looks at me. 'Come on clean yourself'. I cannot move. He pulls down my trousers and shorts. He takes them off over my shoes. He wipes me clean. I cannot move. I cannot speak. It's like I am in a deep water tank where the pressure is so high it is crushing me and this boy is operating mechanical arms from outside. *How can he move? How can he speak? So easily?*

He puts a change of clothes on me. I still cannot move. The soiled ones are put in a bag and are to be brought home and cleaned. The school ones are to be brought back tomorrow.

We walk back to class. The stones on the tarmac slip away underfoot. The sun shines down. Thoughts like fists barrage my head.

■T5: Open Defecation

Why? Why? Feelings likes sharp tooted mouths jump up and grab the thoughts and say, that's why?

I feel warmth in the freedom of the short passage between here and there. I take a sideways look at the play yard through the black metal gate, it is empty and quiet. We enter again the classroom. I sit down and stare straight into the distance again. I won't need to go to the toilet again, I hope.

■ T6: Breaking Cover

The bell rings for playtime. My insides ring too. I have prayed every night to be able to talk. I have prayed to make some friends just to get through the yard play time.

I silently join in the movement of the class as they noisily push back their desks and seats and rush for the door to end their cooped up lesson learning. I pretend to be racing for the door too. I was also pretending that I was comfortable sitting there in class. *I will speak I will not stick to the wall for everyone to look at.*

The door everyone is heading towards is open. Sunlight angles in. A teacher stands at the edge ushering us all out. The children at my front, to my side and from behind rush to the door and out. I see them disperse at the top like water from a spray hose. *I wish I were a droplet of water and not have to think where to go.* I walk through and out into the open space.

Do not go to the wall. I walk. Over there, to where there's people. I stand at the fringe where backs are turned. I pretend to be a part of. I move over there where there's a clear space. I turn and walk over there where there are steps. The steps are crowded with people. I stand at the steps. I try to look like I'm part of the steps crew. The steps are being used as a safe place in a game of tag. Children flit past me in all directions. *Do they think I am part of their game I hope they don't tag me I can't be on what would I do.* I move away. I move over there where there's a loose group. I try and lose others vision of me in

■T6: Breaking Cover

the looseness of the group. *I wish people would stop moving.* I keep moving. My purpose is to keep away from the gravitational pull of the wall, moving here, then there, to and away. I walk across the yard. *This will be different I will talk I walk back across the yard I will talk I'm away from the wall I'm out there.* I feel like I am in that nightmare I have where I let go of the window ledge and fall. I am in no mans' land circling and waiting for the bang of the end. I walk from here to there and back again and back again. No sound passes my lips.

There is a bike shed over there. Children huddle in there in groups. To enter is like a statement that you are going to speak to whoever is in there.

It begins to rain. Everyone races in the direction of the shed for shelter. I follow. My clothes get wetter and wetter. First it is only dots of rain, I can handle that. As the rain gets heavier my clothes get more noticeably wet. *They will wonder why I don't run. Why don't I just come into the shed and out of the rain?* I walk. I feel the urge to run, but don't. Others run past me. I raise my head to avoid the eyes of those in the shed. *If I run now they will wonder why I didn't run before.* The rainwater spatters off the top of the aluminum roof and over the sides of the overfull gutters and cascades down in splashing waterfalls. The shed is full of children escaping the deluge. I see heads turning quickly as spray from striking rain sometimes catches them unawares. I approach and stand at the verge, just underneath the eaves, the rain falls close, vertically down, it's still getting me but at least I'm not out there. A jostle in the crowd causes me to be pushed

Persona Medusa

out into the down pour. I feel the drops hit my head and roll down my cheeks. I turn around to gain my spot back but there is somebody there. I stand on the outside in the rain, beside the occupying presence. I want to say excuse me but I don't, I can't. I wait and wait and wait pretending to enjoy the rain as I get wetter and wetter, nobody moves, my lips don't move. The rain stops and the sun comes out. I stand wet.

In the corner of the playground there are steps down into a basement entrance. A wall surrounds the pit. The pit is dirty and smelly and is in effect used as a bin by everyone. I see there is a chase happening through the playground. A group comes running towards me. I am in the middle of them. There are others ushering them forward and others at the side. I'm not part of this but I can't get free. It's a relief from standing and walking the playground though and my imaginary guards surround me again. We're all led down the dark slimy steps. There's a rotten smell in here. I look up and see the feet of our captors. I have seen people in the dungeon before and have never wanted to be in here. It is always the un-cool who are put in. Every few minutes another body is thrown skidding down the steps. Finders scour the play-yard grabbing others whether they're playing or not and throw them into the hole. I feel less self conscious down in this pit. At least I am part of something here. I am shoulder to shoulder with the other captured kids.

I do not fear the dungeon. I know I'll be released. The thing I fear is the moment of release when everyone is expected to celebrate by

■T6: Breaking Cover

running and screaming away. I cannot do this. The end of play time is coming. I feel like I've been down here for ages. I want to get back up. There is people spitting down on top of us and throwing rubbish. The bell rings. A change is happening. The guards at the top step leave and everyone rushes up the steps and runs screaming away into the playground. I move in that direction, feigning excitement, I dread the top and the release. My eyesight comes level with the tarmac floor of the play yard. Children's feet run there. I leave the coolness and darkness of the dungeon behind. I ascend the steps one by one in the midst of the screaming and movement of the other children. I reach the top and the open tarmac sprawl is laid out before me. The children run and disperse and scream into the open area. I walk slowly and continue walking and then to circling. I walk to the line.

T7: Flickering Fires

The class is very noisy. Children all around me shout and turn and scream. Some are even out of their desks. *Extraordinary*. I am a square peg in this round hole of rambunctious communication. The teacher announces quiet time. 'Silence in the courthouse, Silence in the street, the biggest fool in Ireland is just about to speak, Speak fool speak.' I'm pretty sure it won't be me. We all put our heads down on our arms on the table and go quiet. I peer out through the fold in my arm like a bear in a cave. I see the teacher busily correcting out work at the top of the class. I see all the other children at their desks. They look like question marks. I feel warm. The expectation to speak is gone from me.

Teacher picks up a book. 'Quiet Please. It's Story Time'. My cold stone becomes warm and heats up my body. My brain thaws. The class listens engrossed in the teacher's words and I am part of the whole. There is no expectation to speak here.

I wander around the playing field. I stand between trees. There are lads playing football. *Maybe I can watch these until the bell rings I could play better than them.* I imagine running out onto the pitch grabbing the ball weaving in and out and around everyone and scoring a goal. I stay put. There are some of my class mates playing in the sand pit over there. I wander in that direction. They are playing long jump. I stand and watch. They beckon me over. 'Would you like to have a go?' I nod. I run and hit the marker and jump. Sunlight flits

■T7: Flickering Fires

through the gaps in the black railing that surrounds the playing field. I pass through the air my feet freed from the ground. I feel warm. I land in the sand with a whump. Sound escapes from me. 'Beat that!' I rush back over to the starting line and wait my turn again. For the first time during school break I have spoken. The lunch break passes quickly. *Is this what school is like for everyone else this is great.* The bell rings for the resumption of class. I depart from the sand pit, find my line and wait for the school doors to open. In my mind I am still in the sand pit.

There are lads playing handball up against a big windowless flat wall. I watch from the side passing the time until break ends. The match ends. 'Who's next?' I step forward to my astonishment. He spots me immediately and points. 'All-right DJ'. He wallops the ball up onto the wall with his closed fist. I don't know how he does that. Surely the ball would go crooked. The ball comes back off the wall. I hit it with my open psalm. It strikes the wall and comes back. I feel warm. We to and fro until I run to hit the ball and stumble and miss. I smile and walk back to the side lines. *Do other people feel this great all the time?*

The teacher asks me to read out loud in front of the class. I stand up and read. Nobody seems too bothered that I am speaking. I feel great when in the middle of it, when after the first word is spoken the flow begins. I finish my piece, sit down and re-submerge into silence.

■ T8: Dominance

The person I sit beside in class has taken my book. He's reading it beside me. I want to ask for it back, tell him to give it back but I can't. I stare at my copy book hoping that no one will notice. The teacher finishes reading out the page. 'Next page'. There is a sound in the class of thirty children moving their page in unison. I hope nobody notices that I have no page to turn. I move my eyes sideways. I can just about make out what is written in my book that my neighbor has. *Maybe I can get through this situation by pretending that I forgot my book and that I'm sharing with my neighbor that might make me look cool he's so laid back he doesn't even remember to bring his book in with him.* The teacher starts to move around the class room. She's at the other side now but is coming in this direction. I frantically think of what to do. I remember like a shotgun blast that my name is on my book that my neighbor has. *If the teacher sees my name on my book that my neighbor has and me pretending that I don't have a book I will look weak he has your book why don't you ask for it back.* I can't let my neighbor know I'm looking into my book that he has taken or he will turn it away from me. I write in my copybook. The teacher is standing over me. 'And where's your book?' 'Did you forget it?' 'You'll have to share with your neighbor'. My neighbor with a smile puts my book that he has in the middle our desk. I look down at the words and the page number. I am lost. As soon as the teacher leaves he moves the book away again. I reach over and grab my book. He

■T8: Dominance

tugs it away from me. He looks incredulous at me as if to say 'how dare you'. I want to say that's my book, but can't get the words out. I turn my head and look at the book that he has now placed on his side of the desk. 'What are you gawking at?' He takes my eraser and writes on it the word Zombie. He takes my copy book and writes on it the word Zombie. He whispers in my ear 'I'm glad I'm not you, Zombie'. I turn back into my copybook.

A face confronts me. Our foreheads touch. Eyes stare into my eyes. Hands reach out and shove me. I stumble backwards. My confronter moves towards me. My arm shoots out automatically to try and grab something to stop from falling or to break my fall. I right myself. His face is in my face again. He shoves me. He is strong. He plays football. I can see the muck falling off the base of his boot as the ball goes over the bar for a point. I have always dreaded being asked to fill out the score-sheet for the football as I've never been able to ask how many points a goal is worth. 'Dummy'. He laughs in my face. *Is anyone looking at this? I hope not.* I am moving backwards. *I must not fall.* I focus on not tripping on any of the school bags that lay haphazard on the ground. To fall would be the ultimate defeat. 'Go on do something, Dummy'. I shake my head. He walks back to his desk laughing and shaking his head. I sit back down at my desk.

I'm on my way to the toilet during break time. I can only go to the urinal as if I go to the bowl people will wonder why I didn't ask to go during class. There are two boys standing in my way. I want to tell them to get out of my way but I can't. I try to move around them but they move to block me. They've got their arms folded and are grinning. 'What's the magic word?' 'You're not passing until you say the magic word'. The lesser embarrassment would be to say the magic word but I can't. I move the other way to try and get around. They move to block me. I notice other people are watching. I don't try again. I wait. One of the boys pushes me backwards. I move backwards. I will not fall. They both move off.

I go to the urinal. I stand in between the huge bull nosed urinals with boys coming and going either side of me. *Do they know me am I expected to speak here.* I'm afraid of the noise my water will make when it hits the urinal. This release I think is an extension of my-self. I wait until the boys beside me finish. In this brief interim before that space is occupied again I let go my piss.

I see the cubicle. It looks like a safe place. If I go in there people might wonder why I didn't ask to go during class. I still need to go. It's not too bad. I do the calculations in my mind. *If it's not too bad then I didn't need to ask in class to go to the toilet so it would not look out of the ordinary to go in there now.* I go in and shut the door. I drop my pants and sit on the toilet. I can hear people outside. They are moving around. There is a gap underneath the door, at the top of the door and at the top and bottom of both walls. It's not the safest place away from the gazers in the world. I ponder letting go but imagine the strike when it hits the water as a bomb going off and my location being broadcast all over the toilet area. I hold it. I wait I get conscious of the fact that I'm in here too long. A head appears over the door, grin-

T8: Dominance

ning, pointing, another head appears, grinning, pointing. 'There he is'. 'Are you going to talk now?' 'Say go away'. I don't. I sit and stare at the face of the door. There's writing there. I pretend to read it as if I don't care about the two bobbing heads above me. I hope my name doesn't appear on the door. They throw toilet roll in on top of me. I'm stuck to the pot. The inverted force of nature has me in its grip again. They leave laughing. *Ignore and they'll go away.* It's not an ignoring to me though. It's more like their presence causes this white water geyser which fills my entire being. I let go, wipe and walk out.

It is the break between classes. I sit there silently as the others chat and shout and move about. There is a pair of lad's mess fighting close to me. They are practicing moves from the World Wrestling Federation as they've seen on the television. They are perilously close to me. The teacher walks into class. Most of the students return to their desks. The wrestler is still in the row beside my desk. He raises his arms in the air and shoots out with his right foot while simultaneously doing a small jump in to the air. He catches me on the side just below my ribs with a full force kick. I was not expecting this at all. The pain is real. *No.* Others in the class have seen it too. I can see it on their faces. They watch me expecting a reaction. They get none. I stare straight ahead as the pain engulfs me. The time to react was when the kick struck. It is too late now.

■ T9: Defending Territory

'Pull on the ball!'

'Hook him!'

'Ah for jaysus sake!'

'Open your eyes ref!'

'Square it!'

'Over the bar!'

I see the sliotar curving through the air in my direction. I pull back my hurl and swing. I catch the sliotar perfectly. It heads purpose filled into the top corner of the net. A feeling takes over my body. I am warm from foot to head and buzzing. I feel like my heads going to explode. I don't know how to react. I turn and walk away. My team mates jump around me. I feel bloody great.

'Square ball'

'Yessssssssss'

My local hurling team has just won the county final. We must head off now to a different town to compete in the under 18s all Ireland finals. It's a two night stay with temporary foster parents. I have to go.

I crouch over in the shower, watch as the water bounces off my body and disappears down the plughole. The longer I stay in here the less I'll be out there. I clutch my stomach. I stare at the white floor of the bath. Small bubbles form there. I wish I could up-heave this sugary feeling and watch it disappear down that plughole.

T9: Defending Territory

I have been to all the games, out there on the field with Hurley in hand, battling, clashing, and marking. I do actually enjoy the moments of involvement, when in the heat of battle I lay down my paralysis of movement and fight for the sliotar and try to deliver it to a teammate or in the direction of the goal. My coach says there's less danger of getting hurt if you get stuck in. He's right.

The bus murmurs at the side of the footpath outside the Hurling Park. Parents and players gather around. Excitement knifes the air. Bags are thrown into the undercarriage. Goodbyes are waved and kisses exchanged.

I get on the bus quickly. I need to get a seat before I have to sit beside anyone else. If someone sits beside me then it is their decision. *What do you want me to do about it?*

On arrival each person is assigned a foster family for the weekend. My name is called out and I walk over to my new family. I feel like a shaken fizzy drink can.

Talk, talk, talk please this is it this is the time to change nobody knows you here. I say a few words to my adopted brother on the way to my new home. 'Nice car'. It is a parked BMW. I had heard they were a good car. I congratulate myself. It wasn't even a question. It was an out there observation that any listener could grab upon and respond if they wanted to. 'What?' 'Nice car' 'Where?' 'Back there' 'Oh Yeah, I guess so'. He kicks a tin can out of his way. *Wow I'm nothing short of a raconteur he's not saying much and I'm saying a lot.*

Persona Medusa

We arrive at the house. It's a townhouse, cozy with a solid fuel stove.

I sit down on a seat beside the stove. It reminds me of sleep over's in my Grannies house. We used to stay up late watching RTE1 and eating tonnes of buttery toast and drinking tea. They were enjoyable times until the tipper truck of dung experience could hold no more in and up-tipped it's load on to my home life.

I answer when spoken to here. 'Would you like some tea' 'Yes, please' I congratulate myself on saying the please. It prolongs my speaking that little bit longer. *Hopefully I'll escape the dreaded Q word.*

My adopted sister turns to me. 'You know I've met lots of people, but you're by far the quietest I've ever met'. The thin bough of hope I am sitting on breaks and I fall. I am a cup of sugary scalding tea. These words more than anything else crush me. I am driven back-wall-wards.

Some of the other players from my team are going out for something to eat that evening. I had overheard it being mentioned in the group I was standing beside. *Did that invitation extend to me?* I refuse dinner. *I'm too cool to eat inside I'm going to the diner like I seen in the movies.* I leave the house. 'I've got to meet some friends for something to eat'. It is as hard to stay in the house as it is to go out. *What if I don't get food what will I do then?*

I walk down the street fully hoping not to see anyone I know. In the distance I see familiar faces. My heart thumps. I approach the

■T9: Defending Territory

group and stand on the periphery. Some people turn and salute me. I nod my head in return. *Does that mean I'm part of this group now?* 'We'll go to the chipper down the road for something to eat.' *Who am I going to sit beside what will I get how will I order I'll have to rummage around for change am I even invited.*

The group breaks off into smaller divisions, twos, threes, fours and one. *I have to try I must.* I walk beside a group of three people, listening to the conversation, waiting for an opportunity to get my speak in though I know it's futile. They talk. I walk. They talk about me. It is not nice what they say. I can't respond. They laugh. I am a crushed fizzy drink can. I slow down and let the others move ahead. I don't know where else to go so continue alone along behind the others. *Why won't this end?* I slow down further and further. The chipper is akin to death to me. I trail away and go to my temporary home. I have some sandwiches in my bag and I content myself with eating these in secret.

I enjoy the matches. I can sit and watch. There is something for me and others to be looking at. I don't get to play. Players who I once thought of as talented are demolished by the opposition.

A fellow player takes a huge dislike to me. He whispers in my ear. 'Go home'. I imagine repeatedly smacking him with the edge of my Hurley but cannot even move my mouth.

I am invited out for a drink with my foster brother and sister. The thought of going out fills my blood with sugar. I sip on a tin of beer in a bar looking at my foster brother and sister playing pool. My

Persona Medusa

foster sister starts canoodling with her boyfriend. He comes over to me and says. 'I hear you're the quietest person in the world'. I continue to sip my drink. I imagine the tin rim to be a shield between his words and me as I upturn it into my mouth. I nod. The drink does nothing for me. I don't even know what it's meant to do. I don't even know what's wrong with me that I want fixed.

I walk towards home with my foster brother. On the way we bump into a few of his friends. 'How ya Horse?' They head down a dark alley for a cigarette. 'See you back at the house'. I am relieved.

I walk back to the house. I am an expanded fizzy drink can again waiting for the next crush. Thoughts like black snapping mouths feed on my sugary feeling and grow larger and sharper. I caress the snapping thoughts until they subdue and I can handle them. *Time heals all wounds I wish I could jump into a bath of time.*

Another trip has been organized, a trip to Croke Park in Dublin to see our County team playing against Dublin as a reward for winning the county final and competing in the All Ireland club championship. I've seen pictures of Croke Park. It rises above the surrounding houses. It looks from above like a big eye. It holds tens of thousands of seats and all those seats hold tens of thousands of people. I'm going to be one of them people. There is no way out of it. *I wish we had never won the county final what's it going to be after this a gala dinner in the local hotel where we have to dress up in suits.*

I am up high, looking down. I feel like I could float away into the open space in front of me. My team mates are to the left of me. I al-

T9: Defending Territory

ways try to sit on the edge at least there's not two people I can't speak to. The band plays Amhran Na bhFiann. I stand up with sixty thousand spectators and move my mouth. I feel the hair on my skin standstanding on end.

The game begins. I am stuck. All those eyes, thousands upon thousands *let go let go let go*. There is a huge roar and people jump up clapping and shouting when the other team scores. *What will I do if my team scores? I hope they don't score*. It is easier for me to act disappointed than to act ecstatic.

My team scores a point. My teammates beside me and the thousands of other supporters jump to their feet bashing the air with their fist clenched hands. 'Yeeessssss!' I rise with the rest of them. It feels good to move. I raise my head to see over the person in front of me and clap. Clapping is the easiest show of appreciation there is for me. I sit back down.

A pigeon flies from the rafters across the gigantic space. I wish I could be that free.

◼ T10: Masking Scent

My bicycle is my best friend. I use it to flee home to safety from the school break, have a quick sandwich and then cycle back again. I dread the rain now because it means that I cannot cycle home and if I do and arrive home wet through my parents would wonder why I could not just stay in. Hop onto the saddle. Peddle away. Disappear.

There is an Irish class at the end of every Wednesday and this is followed by a double class of PE. The lads in the Irish class have gotten into the habit of lining their desks up against the back of the wall in a long row as the teacher has not got much authority. This is absolutely dreadful for me. I cannot do this. I have never spoken to any of my classmates. The feeling is still there, waiting for the expectation and the thought to speak and then spear me. I remain where I am in my desk at the top of the class as all the other desks are screeched to the back. A gap opens up behind me. All the lads behind me are laughing and shouting. I am the only one up at the front. I am absolutely exposed again.

I feel a whish over my head. Somebody has just thrown something at me. It whisks up my hair as it shoots overhead. 'Did somebody dig that fella up from the grave?' I do wish the ground would open up and swallow me. I try to turn my head to see who said that but my neck doesn't respond. *What would I do anyways if I did see who threw it imagine beating them up I'm sure they'd give a toss?*

■T10: Masking Scent

I look out of the window and down onto the ground. I see my bike there standing in the rack. *Anymore I'm just leaving.* This thought strikes home. I feel warm. I have just made a decision, a decision to run, but a decision nonetheless. *I will leave after this class and skip PE altogether.*

Seen by anyone who looks I bend down at my bike, open the lock, clasp my hands around the handle bars, hoist it away from the rack, casually wheel it off the premises, expecting somebody to grab me and question me but nothing. I lift my leg over the saddle and cycle away. The relief to be leaving such a nightmare existence behind is enormous to me. I imagine the others heading down to the PE hall, togging out and heading off to the football pitch to kick a ball around and I feel the air passing my head as I cycle myself away from this. To know that I have the power to do what I want gives me strength. *I'm sick of this I'm leaving end of story.*

I cycle the road home. *Where to go to not be seen I hope my parents don't pass.* The bushes on either side of me are wavering in the breeze. The chestnut trees are heavy with their load. I pass the haunting earth of the graveyard. My heart quickens at the thought of an under earth soul appearing in front of me or behind me and tapping me on the shoulder. The road disappears under the front wheel of my bike as I carry on forward. I cannot go home. I take a turn down the narrow road to where the lake lays. I cycle in line with the flowing river. I watch as it lazily ripples towards its gathering point. I stop at the bridge and watch the river flow under. I cannot actually see under

Persona Medusa

the bridge. *This might be a good spot to hide.* I un-mount from my bike and hide it as best I can in the bushes. I consider for a moment bringing it under the bridge with me but imagine it falling into the water and then me jumping in after it and drowning. That would be embarrassing. I clamber down the slope and under the bridge.

Dark rippling shadows bounce off the cool stone curvature of the underside of the bridge as the river passes through. An occasional fish flits by. The stones underneath the water are smoothed by the flows touch. River weed trails in the flows wake clutching to the stones. A breeze comes down along the river gently rustling the reeds and caressing my skin.

I sit, my bicycle lying at my side, and take in the beauty that I lay surrounded within. I read a book, 'Hard Times' by Charles Dickens, it is for my English class. I feel warm. I am at one with nature. I soak in the written words.

The snapping snout still finds me here though at times. A car approaches and passes. Voices approach and pass. I imagine what would happen if someone sticks their head in under the bridge out of curiosity. *Would they have been expecting to find a cowering creature beneath? Would they take a quick glance then look quickly away? Would they look back again? Would they ask what am I doing under there?* I have an answer prepared. *I'm studying for my exams. It's quieter out here.*

I move away from under the bridge. I've started picturing myself as a troll. I climb a gate walk through a field and find the railway

■T10: Masking Scent

tracks. I climb up the embankment and hide in the long grass or amongst a small grouping of trees. I think back to when I was little. I used to come here with my Dad and roll down the embankment with the sound bouncing out of me at every roll.

I hear voices coming from the railway. I take a peek over the long grass. They have high-vis jackets on with Iarnroad Erireann written on them. I stop what I'm doing and stay perfectly still as the voices approach then dissipate again into the distance as they walk on by.

I imagine myself as Huckelberry Finn. I stretch out on the grass. The glorious sunshine warms me. Through blades of grass I see a barbed wire fence, trees stately and plump, bushes fluttering. I pull my head back and see the sky a blue sphere perfectly overhead with birds soaring and plummeting.

I wonder about the duel aspects of my life so far. *How can I be as comfortable in nature as this and then turn to stone whenever another person enters my world?*

T11: Rickety Bridge

I sit in the exam hall. It is the last exam of my schooling. I have brought plenty of pens in case I run out and would have to raise my hand and ask for a spare pen. My stomach is loudly growling. *I should have eaten more.* It is the most noise I have ever made in school. *Can other people hear?* I look around the hall, everyone has their heads down. No-one seems to notice my growling rumbling noises. The supervisor hands me the paper. I know there won't be any unexpected expectations to speak here and I feel warm. I will take my time and be sure not to be last or first to finish and head out the door. To be first would draw too much attention to those still taking their tests and to be last runs the risk of there being groups formed and hanging around outside.

I put my head down and read and write. The words come easy. It is all written. Interspersed with my thoughts on the exam in front of me there are thoughts of what I'm going to do when the exam is finished. *How am I going to avoid the after exam expected party?* I see some students finish and leave boldly out the door *I hope they're not going to hang around.*

I finish. I look around to make absolutely sure nobody else is finishing at the same time as I. I push back my seat and walk up to the supervisor's desk. I leave my papers in and walk out the door. The cold feeling comes into me as I imagine there being a gang of people on the other side of the door. I imagine them looking wide eyed to see

T11: Rickety Bridge

who it is and ask how it went and on seeing that it's me turning away and back into their group. There is nobody here. I walk quickly down the corridor dreading every corner. I reach the front door, push it open and walk out. The summer sun is in full shine. I enjoy the warmth on my skin. I wrestle with my bicycle lock like I'm in a horror film and I'm trying to start the car while a pack of Zombies are heading in my direction. Nobody else comes out the door. *Thank God.* I depart slowly wary of those that have already left. I don't want to bump into them. I feel a wave of excitement. *I'm finished.* I take a look over my right shoulder at the face of the place which for some reason crushed my voice. *What comes next though?*

I have no-where else to go except home. I am acutely aware of this. This is one of them times that everyone is meant to go out with their friends and celebrate. It is the finish of school. I do not have anyone. I am expected to go to a bar and talk and shout with my classmates. I do not understand what alcohol is meant to do. I remember the last time I drank I clutched a table as my vision behaved like an old TV set with the picture moving up the top and reappearing at the bottom over and over. I imagine how I'm going to get around this without telling my parents that I've been mute in school for the last thirteen years and cannot speak to these people who have witnessed it. *Pretend to go out but actually hide in the field.* I try to run with the thought of actually going out but the thought runs off a cliff and I stare into space. At least the feeling doesn't come up to bite me. The front wheel of my bike hits a pothole and I curse out loud where only the trees and the birds can hear.

Nobody rings me to go out which isn't surprising as nobody has my number. I have already made my excuses as too why I'm not going out. It isn't because I have no friends. I tell my Mam that everyone else finished the day before but I had to wait and do my art exam which was an add-on to the normal exams and I really wanted to go out too. I had actually done art classes every weekend for the past year for this exact reason. I sit in the garden. The suns heat washes over me. A grasshopper ticks in the grass. The future enters my mind. It troubles me. *What next can it be any different?* I think about the results. H*ow will I get out of going out when the results come in I'll have to go out.*

It is results day. I am doubled over in my bedroom. I feel as if there is a second mouth inside me eating up my intestines. It's doing a lot more work than my real mouth ever did. I am worried not about the results but about the expected after party. I managed to get out of the party at the finish of the exams with a plausible excuse. There is no excuse I can think of for this one. I must follow on the wave of excitement.

I get up on my trusty bike and cycle slowly towards the school. The school comes into view followed by familiar faces that I had never been able to speak too. I approach slowly as slow as I can go. I pass by the assembled groups, park my bike between two metal rods, get off and walk in through the main door. The secretary hands me an

T11: Rickety Bridge

envelope, anticipation and self consciousness attack me. I am afraid to open it, afraid that if it is very good then I'd be expected to shout or scream with joy and it is impossible for me to do that and then if other people were to see my very good result they would think me an unresponsive, ungrateful, never happy individual for not whooping with joy. I half hope the results are bad. Bad news is easier to react to. I rip open the small brown envelope, pick out its contents, I am happy, one A, a few Bs, a couple of Cs. A fellow comes over and asks how I have done. His eyes pop out. 'An A in English, your parents will be happy'. My English teacher comes over and says 'Congratulations'. It is the first time a teacher has spoken to me as a human being.

I circle the groups of people. Everyone is making plans to go out for a drink. I feel the teeth closing on me. *I must get out of here but I need to know at least where the party is I need something to tell my parents maybe if I got worse results I would have an excuse not to go out.* I want to fit in, especially now. *Maybe if I have one good day it would make up for the last thirteen years of being between the teeth of the school beast.* A fellow must be organizing things, goes around to each group saying, eight o clock in the bar. I am standing close to one of the groups and hear this. *That means I'm invited too.* I get on my bike and leave.

I am delighted with my results but I have no doubt that going out is going to be a social nightmare. I begin to desperately think of ways out of it. I arrive home and show my results around. My parents are impressed. I have received enough points to take my choice of study in college.

It's four O' Clock. *Only four hours left until death.* I walk outside. I sit in the sun. I go back inside. I sit in my room. Humiliations from the past reach in and twist my intestines. My intestine noose gets tighter and tighter as the minutes ceaselessly pass by. I try to remain calm. I dress myself up in a shirt and jeans. It is too early. They might as well have been made from thistles. My eyes focus on the distance scanning for the danger. I know the inevitability of what will happen. I walk through the living area, say goodbye to my parents and head out to my bike. I'm taking my bike because I'm still thinking of taking a detour to the lake and hiding out there. I cycle into town and walk to the bar.

I open the door, a wave of noise and smoke hit me. I let go the door and walk into its midst. I do not see anyone I know. M*aybe they're not here maybe it's called off am I even invited.* I breathe a premature sigh of relief. I continue walking deeper into the bowels of the bar. I use people I don't know as shields from those I know. Once someone I know sees me I know I will turn to stone. These people I don't know are moving statues that I don't expect to speak to me or me to have to speak to them. I see my classmates at the far-end of the bar. I side step so my view is blocked by another person. I try to gather some resolve. There is none. I have for all accounts never spoken in school to these people. They are talking animatedly. I approach the group. I have not seen many people drunk before. They seem looser,

T11: Rickety Bridge

but still I feel uncomfortable. A face turns around. 'I heard you did well on your exams?', 'Yeah, all right'. As I say my little sentence, my mind races with thoughts of how to add to it to continue this conversation. 'How did you do?', 'Oh not so bad, not as good as you though'. My mind runs out of traction and heads off the cliff. *Hang onto this fellow so I don't drift off into space I have to get a drink though why is he speaking to me?* I leave my anchor on the outskirts of the group and approach the bar. The bar is very loud and I worry the barman won't hear me and I'll have to repeat and repeat and I imagine him handing me a piece of paper to write my order down on and all the auld fellows looking at me wondering what degree of specimen is this that is coming up after them. I order a pint of stout and congratulate myself. I have a couple of minutes wait when it settles. My back is a shield against the sounds coming from behind me. My drink turns from creamy white to black and the barman tops it up. I hand over my money. I take a sip to prolong turning around. I take another sip. *Where will I go when I turn around?* I reel my eyes in from the distance and focus on the beer taps with their lighted labels. I turn.

I walk towards the huddles of my classmates. I walk here and to there. I lift my drink to my mouth and sip. My drink is a shield. It isn't making me feel any different. When the glass is in my mouth and the liquid flowing down my throat I know I am not expected to speak. Between sips the sounds of intermingled talk packs at my ears, bits and pieces make it as far as my brain. When I think of something to say to break into a group I feel a rush like a fountain of sugar. By

Persona Medusa

the time the rush finishes the moment is gone. I take another sip as if to dampen this sugar. The longer I stand in sipping silence the harder it becomes to actually to say anything. *What am I doing? This is just like the playground I thought I wasn't going to do this again why don't I do as I say?*

I don't want to leave but I must. This is getting embarrassing again. The words from my hurling coach come back to me. *Get stuck in it's the only way not to get hurt.* I never shouted for the ball on the field of play or spoke to my team mates there either. How can I say goodbye when I've barely said hello. To draw attention to myself that I am here when I feel that I'm not here is unthinkable. I wait and sip and start to plan my exit. *Just turn and leave no there would be more classmates further to the front of the bar and I'd have to pass these and explain why I'm leaving no.* My glass is nearing empty. I imagine going to the bar and ordering another, waiting, thinking, turning. *Hang onto my nearly empty glass until I find an opportunity to leave.* I feel nothing different from this drink. The public house is getting further full. I am jostled as I stand with no anchor. Smoke is building up. I spot a place to leave my glass down. I raise it to my mouth and take an exaggerated nonchalant swig. I place it down and move through the throng. My formative years have not been very informative

I walk through the town, knowing and feeling that I will soon be out of this place. I examine the shapes of anyone who appears into my sight. I feel relief when I don't recognize them. I reach my trusty bike

◾T11: Rickety Bridge

and bend down to undo the chain. *I've made it.* I imagine my parents asking why I am home so early. I think of what to say. *I just had a couple of pints and left maybe if I cycle slowly I can burn up time and it will look like I stuck around for more than one drink but I better move from here before I bump into anyone.*

I cycle along the celestial lit country road. The green bushes rustle on either side. Cars blind me with their full headlights and then dim. *I must exist if they're dimming for me.* I try to cycle slowly but there is only so slow I can go without falling. *Don't fall under a car that would be embarrassing.* My bike wobbles and I end up in the ditch on the other side of the road. I laugh.

I reach home. I walk into the house where my parents are watching TV. 'How'd it go', 'Fine', 'You're home early', 'Yeah, oh I just had a couple of pints and left, you know'.

I lay on my bed feeling the alcohol take effect. The room spins around. I hold onto the bed and clutch at the sheets. I have in my hands a plastic shopping bag. I roll over and puke into this. *If only I could speak with such relief and power I should get up and bring it to the bin.* I fall asleep.

◾ T12: Wetlands

I have a summer job, manually cultivating the peat sod. I pray that I will talk here away from the familiar and expecting faces of school. I pray that there are no witnesses from school here.

I approach an old farmhouse. An unfriendly to stranger's dog darts at me with menacing mouth open yelping and drooling and shaking his dirty shaggy body. I try not to look afraid as there are the people I will be working with over there by the steps over the wall which leads to the railway line and the bog stretch. A rope tied to the dog's collar stops him in his tracks. I think I'm okay. That was real danger for the length of his leash. I walk over to the crew. There are four people there of my own age. None of them know me. This is a clean break from school. I will speak I re-tell myself. 'Hi'. I congratulate myself. My sugar geyser subsides. 'Hi'. We clamber over the dripping with dew timber steps and onto the sunlight glinting railway tracks. *I spoke I spoke I'm part of this group now Speak, Speak, More, Please.* I can see them moving away from me. Our breaths are held suspended in the cold morning air. Coming into view is a bridge across a lazily flowing river slicing through the morning mist. Slow, calm, graceful, it doesn't care what we think or do. It does its own thing. *What will we do if a train comes oh sure we would have seen or heard it before we started crossing the bridge.* The track runs across the bridge and there are stones underneath the track and built up on

T12: Wetlands

the edges. A half a mile the other side of the bridge and the bog comes into view. It is a vast flat expanse of peat turf.

I meet the boss who shows me to the starting point. I stand at the start of a long row of stacked wet turf about six sods high. It stretches further than I can see. All these sods have to be turned and stacked again in a new row to dry in the summer sun.

There is only one thing to do. I get down on bended knees and begin. I rip and peel the one wet slushy mud stuck sod from another and lift and move and place on to the dry ground beside me for it to dry and be harvested. Within the working movement I think I need things to change. I imagine each sod I pull up is a bad memory that I drag out of my head and leave under the sunlight to be lighted, warmed and burned.

The first break is coming up. It's a short break. *I should go over to where my work mates are*. I look over. They don't seem to be moving towards each other. *Too far away maybe it's only a short break I'll just sit where I am and eat my sandwich*. It's like having a gun pointed at my head and thinking the decision to sit still is mine. Tea and sandwiches in the open air, lovely.

The big break arrives, lunch. There's no excuse this time I must go over to where my workmates are. If I don't I may give up completely. I poke my head up beyond the turrets of turf. I see my workmates moving to a singular spot. *Go*. I move across to where the others are sitting in a circle. My hammer thumping heart hammers harder as I get closer. 'Hi'. 'Hi, have a seat'. He points to the bog ground. 'Where are you from?' 'How'd you make it down here?' I answer as quickly as possible and congratulate myself. I know it won't be enough. These questions give me permission to speak. It is free speaking that I have a problem with. I dread these questions. These people don't know how I was in school. They don't know the lack of experience of anything I have because I stayed away from any expectation to speak. The questions cease. The group goes back to its normal free flowing conversation. I can feel my speak slipping away. Words toss in the air around me. People speak without holdbacks. Most times others start speaking before the other is finished. Sometimes there are quick pauses in the talk. The thought to speak comes to me. This is immediately followed by a sugar geyser. This lasts for a second then the silence ends and the conversation moves on. I close my fingers into the soft ground. This feeling is too powerful for me. I am being defeated once again by an inverted primal force of nature. I think of leaving and going back to where I was working but I can't. I would have to announce my departure. If I could do that then I wouldn't have a problem in the first place. I can't announce my departure when I've contributed nothing since my arrival. The thought to speak keeps striking me and is always and immediately followed by the torrent of sugar. I feel the soft ground beneath me. I move my hand and a thistle glints my skin. A bright red bog flower in the distance captures my attention. A long trench filled with murky turf water sits still beside me. The glorious sun drapes me in its warmth. In the middle of all bog beauty I sit still. I am waiting until the dispersion comes. This time at least I am not heading into the playground to wander by myself or heading into the classroom. I have somewhere to go and something to do. *Why do I have to wait for the movement of other people to allow myself to move?* I feel like my stomach has burst and the acid is devouring my intestines. The break ends and we move back to our rows. Back to work.

The sun beats down through a cloudless sky. The rows are finished. There is a small lull in the work as we wait to hear where we are going next. We sit in the shade of the tractor and trailer. I sit beside the wheel of the trailer. My workmates sit in the shade of the larger wheel of the tractor. They talk and laugh. I hear them talking of going for a swim. The river is divinely enticing. I see it through the reeds in the distance. I truly want to go for a swim. I stare at the clumps of dirt on the trailer wheel. I feel the earth rumble when a heavy machine passes by. I look at the wobbling ground. I feel the penetration of voices. I know that if I do not move to join the other group I will be left behind examining the dirt ground beside the shadowing wheel. I will myself immensely. *This is my chance I must move over there I have to speak.* My thoughts are like threads for a rope that forms a noose which gets tighter and stronger the more I think about speaking and freedom. I feel the churning devouring swirl in my stomach. My eyes blur. My co-workers seem a million miles away. I pretend to fold my arms as I clutch my stomach to try and lessen the devouring. I sway forward and backwards. I see the earth. I see the sky. I pretend to be still. I feel a gurgling physical sickness in my stomach. I hold this in as well. Nothing comes out. The mould will not be broke. The decision is made and up they get. I hear them speaking. 'What about him?', 'Leave him'. One looks back at me. I am rocking gently forward and back. 'Are you coming?', 'Nah, I'm fine here'. *Well done you spoke when spoken to.* I continue to rock forward and backward as the group walks towards the rushes hidden river. Their voices grow fainter and fainter. I feel a relief when I realize they are far enough gone that I can move without being seen. I unwrap my arms from around my middle and let myself fall towards the earth. New sounds come, splashing, shouts, screams. I imagine them over there having brilliant fun, undressing, reed caresses on bare skin, bare feet on stone river ground brushed by currents, pushing, falling, underwater, re-emerging. The slight caressing breeze brings these sounds to my ears as I lay sideways on the soft bog ground. The horizon lies high, pushes the sky away. I see more earth than sky.

◼ L1: Cloud over Clearing

It is autumn in the clearing.

I awake in the morning. The sheets are heavier than I remember. A stale smell affronts my nostrils and causes me to recoil. All the bed is wet. I remember at bedtime staying awake as long as possible to keep the morning at bay for the longest possible time. Now it is here and it is smelly and wet. I make the bed hoping that the sheets will dry out by the time I get back to them, anything rather than admission. I cannot get the screams out at night or the words out during the day. My blood is sugar.

I roam in the middle of the playground. I see a figure that I recognize from my other life at home. Someone I can actually speak to. He's smiling at me and moving towards me. I can't smile back. My expression is blank. *What's he doing here?* He stands in front of me. 'Wakey, Wakey'. He waves his hand in front of my face. I can-not speak not even to him, my friend. What comes naturally outside is impossible inside. My outside friend looks on with a bewildered face. 'Cat got your tongue'. He moves away with his friends effortlessly. *Now he knows he will never look the same on me again and I will not be able to speak to him outside of school either.* My blood is sugar.

I sit in the garden of my home in the country. I hear shouts coming from up the road. A group of people come into my view. Some of them I know from school. I hope to hell they do not see me. I do not move. They pass. They're on their way to the lake. There is no where

Persona Medusa

I can go. I wait for the night to come when I know there is only one place to be, in darkness beneath blankets, where no eyes can capture me. My blood is sugar.

A thought out of the blue enters my head. *Will I speak in school tomorrow? Where will I sit? What will I do when school is finished?* I swallow a tonne weight into my stomach and stare into the distance. *Do not let what happens out there invade here.* My blood is sugar.

It is my Birthday. It's family only. Mum Dad and me. I have no one to invite. No one invites me. It has become more noticeable with each passing year. I feel the pain but accept it as part of the weight of this cross I must carry. I sit at the table and eat my cake. Crumbs fall onto the table and I wipe them off the table with one hand and catch them with the other. I put them back on the plate. *I should be out enjoying myself doing whatever people of my age do I don't have a clue.* I can speak here but my voice has become so alien to me that it feels weird to even speak in my own home. Out there is where I need to speak. My blood is sugar.

I watch a football match on the television. I can see the players kicking a ball around. I think back to all the conversations I heard in the school yard centered on football. 'What team do you support?' 'Did you see that goal last night?' I know I can watch the game sitting on the couch at home but I know that I cannot speak about it and the thought that I may have to speak about it is causing the feeling to rise in me again. I look at the television but take in nothing of what's going on. My blood is sugar.

◾ 1.1: Cloud Over Clearing

I read a book. It is to avoid going out there where there are people. I see the words on the page. I can understand them. I know even the simple things in the story I cannot do. The feeling rises in me whenever I read simple statements like, 'he said', 'she said' and 'I asked'. My blood is sugar.

I write a computer game on my Atari. I call it 'Cold Fire'. I stare into the screen typing and typing code. I make a little man run and jump and shoot bullets. *I should be out there drinking and shifting women like I hear other kids talking about doing.* I send my game into a magazine and it gets rejected. This doesn't bother me. I have done something. My blood is sugar.

It is as though I am living my life on an ice plane, a thin veneer of happiness and then the ice breaks and I plunge into an immense depth of freezing darkness. I lash out with arms and legs. I push against the darkness and uplift myself towards the surface light. I clamber over the edge and live on. I leave the darkness where it is to build and build. My blood is sugar.

I go to bed and pray '...*Guard me in the dark of night*....'

It is winter in the clearing.

My haven is gone. I have nowhere to go. I walk around the house. In my sleep I receive nightmares. When I'm awake I think about all the things I should be doing, all the things I will have to do, all the things I can't do. *How can I do these thing I can't speak I am going to be made mincemeat out of in the real world.* How I am at school has permeated in to every other aspect of my life. Thoughts are

Persona Medusa

big black lead shapes that fall on top of any positive rising feeling. My communication has stopped here too.

I go to bed and pray '....*and in the morning send your light, Amen.*'

■ L2: Greener Grass

I knock on the door of my new home for my first year in college. The first day is always the easiest. The door opens and I am welcomed in. They are a small family. The mother shows me around. She mentions that I am sharing a room with another fellow from my hometown. 'Really, what's his name?' I ask like I'm a man about town and know everyone in the town. The name she mentions is a fellow from my class at school. *It couldn't be the same person.* I hope it isn't. I feel it is. I sit and have a cup of tea. I am early. I am always early. I think if I am early I'll have time to talk before the others arrive. I have nothing to base this belief on as so far it hasn't worked for me.

My new room-mate enters. He has taken the late train. I turn slowly from the TV. I know he's a witness. *I've come here to get away from everyone and everything I know and now I'm sharing a room with someone who knows everything.* 'Hi', 'Hi'. We sit at the table. There is no such thing as small talk to me. We talk about our college courses, the trip up, our new lodgings. I don't mention school. I am expected to speak about these things and so I do. It is like reading in front of the class. *Is it the anticipation that gets me like hearing a rustling in the bushes and anticipating a tiger to break loose and come charging at me but then finding out it is just a donkey but still being afraid of the donkey?* I want to say goodnight. I feel that familiar beast grab hold of me. I try to put my voice across the gap but fail.

Persona Medusa

I fall into quietness and stare at the TV. 'I'm off to bed' 'Oh all right'. I follow my past to bed.

The course I have chosen is Quantity Surveying. It had been recommended by my careers guidance counselor. I can see the sense somewhat. It is mostly measuring off drawings, being as meticulous as possible, a good excuse for remaining quiet in front of a computer or with pen and paper all day.

The college lecture rooms are different to the school rooms. I don't have to sit beside the same person every day. I get it into my head that if I can ask a question here, just out of the blue, that I would be on the road to recovery. I am like a panting dog with its mouth shut. The space between the source of my voice and its target seem as great as ever. The feeling remains the same. I try to hide the feelings by acting nonchalantly. I lean back on the hind legs of my seat, look out the window, examine the few women in the class. I comfort myself that not many people ask questions. *Maybe they're like me.* The words of a previous teacher enter my head. *Maybe you'd find something like DJ up there.* He was talking about Mars.

I sit in class dutifully taking notes. A classmate calls across the room to me. 'Hey DJ open the window it's roasting in here'. I tense completely. I was not expecting this. There is a monkey wrench in my cogs. I don't react immediately. Seconds seem like minutes. The whole class is quiet waiting for a reply. I can't give one. I don't like other people telling me what to do but I can't tell them where to go. My heart beats fast. *Is this a challenge?* Someone stirs behind me and

■L2: Greener Grass

goes and opens the window. A brush of cool air comes in and caresses me. *I wish my breath would caress my vocal cords so effortlessly and deliciously* The would be project manager turns away. I can see he's slightly embarrassed and frustrated by my failure to respond to him.

I am in my Land Surveying class. The lecturer asks us to break up into groups of four to carry out a project. My classmates start looking around and gravitating to each-other. I gravitate to no one and no one gravitates to me. I spasm inside. It's like my whole body is one big heart moving in and out faster and faster. *I must get out of here.* Never before have I been able to walk away from a situation like this. I would just stand there frozen. *You're in college now you can do what you want leave.* I see the door out of my blurry vision. I see no one else is looking at me. I remember that the door opens inwards. This is important to me as I don't want to be fumbling at the door and everyone turns around and looks. I walk towards the door. I feel like I'm going to implode. I open the door and walk into the corridor. The corridor looks as if it is melting. I can see through the walls. The corner seems a million miles away *I must move from here before anyone comes out where can I go too early to go back to the digs can't hang around college the toilet.* I walk towards the toilets. They are toilets that my classmates wouldn't normally use. I enter the cubicle. I breathe a sigh of relief. My middle goes up and down like a manic yo yo ball and my blood is full to the brim with sugar. I grasp hold of the toilet pot and bend over. It doesn't help. I crouch down it doesn't help. I don't get sick. I walk in circles. It doesn't help. I wait. *How*

Persona Medusa

long can I spend in here sure how would anyone know. I still wait. I can't meet any of my classmates. *How would I explain why I left the class I don't know what's happening to me.* I sit on the toilet watching my watch as the hours pass by and my body returns to normal.

I sit at the back of class. I look at the people around me. I can see their swords un-sheating. *Time is running out again for me I must speak what is this thing that holds me back.* I feel like there is a missile stuck down my throat programmed to detonate when it reaches the bottom of my stomach. Every-time I swallow it slips further down.

The class ends. A dispersion happens. My nonchalance in class is exposed. It is not so bad if there is a class immediately after. It is when there is a break in classes that I am stumped. The library becomes my refuge. There are newspapers in there for communal reading. I bury my head in there even though I am taking nothing in of what I'm reading. I see the sports page. *That's what I should be reading that would give me something to talk about.* I start to read but my vision gets blurry and I feel my middle tighten and churn. The anticipation about speaking about anything I read here has got me again.

In my bag my uneaten sandwich lays. My digs mother made it for me as part of my rent. *Where will I eat it if I go into the canteen there might be people from my class there if I try to find a seat out in the concourse there will be people from my class there if I throw it in the bin I might be seen or someone will see the sandwich and wonder who put that there I could eat it on the way home but that would spoil*

■L2: Greener Grass

my dinner I could leave it in my bag but it would smell. The words on the newspaper are still a blur.

My college life is turning out to be just the same as school life. I do the same things automatically even though I tell myself repeatedly not to. I walk in circles from here to there and back again, walk down corridors dreading that I might see someone I know, look for escapes, studiously pretending.

At my digs I arrive in. 'Hello'. The hello is getting harder every day. I want to change but this thing is feeding on itself. I don't have anything to talk about from home or college. I wait for dinner, watch TV. Something enters my head to say but I can't just put it out there. I say it over and over in my mind and tell myself again and again to say it but it's like a rolling sugar ball, gathering more and more sugar and then the moment passes and it explodes. I think about changing the channel but I can't just change it without making some comment like 'this sucks let's see what else is on'. The remote lies beside me but I cannot pick it up as to do so would signal that I am going to change the channel and I would have to say what I am going to do. I leave it there and watch whatever is on. My house mate announces he's off to bed 'Goodnight' 'Goodnight' I feel comfortable. I pick up the remote and scan through the channels. I get up and walk around the couch. I have nowhere to go. My only comforts are the in-limbo zones, the walk to college, the walk home from college, the train home.

I think about leaving the educational system. M*aybe I'm institutionalized.* I pass a car garage on the way to college. I hear the lads shouting and laughing. I know I'd be screwed there too. I see homeless people on the street enjoying the warm sunshine of the morning and asking for money off of passersby for drink, maybe a coffee. I'd be screwed there too. I make up my mind to stay the course.

A classmate approaches me, a friendly face. He stands before me asking simple questions and to my immense pride and surprise I find that I am answering easily. There is no sudden change of direction when we catch sight of each-other, no turning of the head when he has something to say and sees it's me beside him. He invites me out to drink with his pals. He invites me to move into a flat with him and a few others from the class.

A warmth washes over me.

■ L3: Gatherer

I am in the flat with my classmates. Eastenders is on the TV. One of my classmates gets up to make tea. 'Anyone for a cuppa?' 'Aye' 'Aye' 'Yeah' 'Yep'. I say yep though I have yet to get up myself and ask if anyone wants tea. I feel guilty about this. The guilt is in the punch ring with the freeze feeling that comes whenever the thought to ask if anyone wants tea comes into my head.

I have brought up a packet of biscuits from home. I have placed them on the corner shelf in the kitchen. The kitchen and the living room are one room in this one bedroom flat. They've been sitting there for the last three days. I've been trying to defeat this freeze feeling whenever I'm expected to speak all that while and the weeks before and ask my class-mates would they like some tea. I dare not even move on the couch for fear of a spring squeaking which would create expectation of a comment or of movement. *Come on you're not in school this isn't the roll call.* I have said no at times when offered a cup of tea though I want a cup of tea just because I don't want it to come across that I am lazy and always take and never give. *I should have said from the start that I didn't drink tea and then only drink it at the weekend at home.* I dare not look at my biscuits. *Maybe I can pretend I've forgotten about them.* I catch a glimpse of them out of the corner of my eye sitting there prominent in that they are not being eaten. *I hope nobody notices maybe I could put them back in my bag and take them away when I'm here by myself.* I curse myself for not

Persona Medusa

having thought of this before I put them up in such a prominent position. *Never again will I make this mistake.*

My class-mate starts handing out the cups of tea. I take hold of mine 'Cheers'. I take a sip. It's hot and milky. 'I don't understand you milky boys'. *My God he didn't comment on the fact I'm not speaking that could easily have been the Q word.* He dances over to where my biscuits are held. He takes them down and proceeds to hand them out. He does this is an exaggerated way. *He knows there mine.* He offers them to me. 'Sure I'll take two seeing as their mine'. My class-mates laugh. I breathe a sigh of relief. *At last that's them biscuits out of the way maybe bringing up the biscuits redeems me for not making tea yet I will make tea tomorrow.* I enjoy my tea and biscuit and the release from prison of my biscuits and my voice.

I am in college trying to study. A construction book is laid out on the desk in front of me. I do not see the words or diagrams on the book. All I am thinking of is. *Today I must make tea.* I have a plan. *I will get up and go to the toilet. I can do this without saying anything though there is that uncomfortable moment when I start to move and people notice me I will then on the way back from the toilet use my momentum and the disturbance caused by my momentum to ask if anyone wants a cup of tea.* My college learning isn't being very enlightening.

I stand in the toilet in the flat. I'm holding my lad over the rim but I don't need to go. *Why? Go in there and make tea.* I wash my hands of course. I come back into the room and stop in the middle. I

■L3: Gatherer

ask falsely nonchalantly. 'Would anyone like a cup of tea?' 'Aye' 'Aye' 'Aye' 'Aye'. As the kettle is boiling I am struck by a dart of a thought. I don't know if they take sugar. *I should know this really if I had been making tea as often as they did I will ask as soon as the kettle finishes boiling.* 'Sugar?' I hand each tea over to each of my flatmates. 'Cheers DJ'. I enjoy the thanks. *Wow I am up making tea for people I am a part of something.* I sit down pleased with myself. *I have done it that's me covered for the next few days at least.*

I take a sip and stretch out my legs. A cup of tea topples over and spills all over the carpet creating a dark wet spot. There is silence. I know I should fill this silence with a 'Fuck' or 'Shit' or 'Sorry' or anything but I don't. I stare at the spilt tea. Everyone else stares at me. I get up and desperately look for something to clean it with. I catch sight of a tea cloth hanging on a hook over the kitchen countertop. I make a beeline for it. Once I have created the disturbance I can speak. 'Sorry'. I grab the tea towel. My flat-mate stops me. 'Hang on there. That comes in handy'. He gets out of his chair and does a little jig stamping his feet on the wet patch and exclaims. 'That's how you get rid of it'. Everyone laughs. I marvel at his initiative. I remake him a cup of tea. I re-sit down on the couch and wait for when it's time for sleep.

I manage to get a part time job to pay for my college. It is in a multi-plex cinema. I am working behind the main counter. *What am I doing?* I look at the long lines of people queuing up for refreshments. There are people everywhere. *Maybe this is what I need to be sur-*

Persona Medusa

rounded by people not to give myself a chance to feel the freeze feeling to submerge myself.

I realize I do not know how to make the popcorn. *I must ask.* The thought to ask raises the freeze feeling in me. I draw in my breath. I have the SOS on the tip of my tongue. The closer I get to speaking the more intense the freeze feeling comes. I let out a voice that is cut off from my body. It is weak. Nobody hears. 'Do you want some help?' 'Yes, please'.

The customers come steadily towards me. I see each one as a gigantic mouth with sharp teeth waiting to close on me. I get over the initial rush. 'Hi. Could I have a medium coke and popcorn please?' I've been told to try and upgrade them to a large coke and popcorn. It's only 50 pence extra. I can do this no problem. I have permission.

I have run out of change. I have to get the attention of the supervisor. I think to shout out, impossible. I think to turn, impossible. A customer buys some popcorn. I don't have the change for her. I now have permission to speak. I turn around and make eye contact with the supervisor. 'I need more change here'.

◼ L4: Watering Hole

I am invited out for drinks with my new flat-mates. We gather around a table in a bar. A round is bought. My asked for drink is placed down in front of me. I drink. I take in my surroundings. *There is five people here including me that means if I wait until the end I'll have four drinks on board before I have to buy a round I wish I could just get up and buy a round now and get it over with but then my turn would come around again too soon no wait till last then when it's my turn again I'll be on my tenth drink and nobody will care.* I drink and listen. I laugh with everyone else when a story is recounted. I actually have only non-stories. My would be stories have all ended prematurely because of my inability to speak to people. *How come I can make noise when I laugh but still can't put my voice out there?* This is the longest I've ever stayed in a bar without the need to escape to limbo coming over me. With each stout down I feel like I actually could speak if I had something to say. The fourth drink lands in front of me. *My round is next.* I sip slowly and watch. I want to remain in tow on the flow. The pints are nearly at their half way stage. *Wait not yet wait wait actually go to the toilet first.* I walk down the stairs to the toilet. It's easy when you have somewhere to go. I can feel my body all over. It is a warm feeling flowing in my blood stream. My feet feel lovely heavy. I lift and drop down the stairs. I stand lovely unsteadily at the urinal trough. *Wow if I'm like this after four pints what will I be like after eight?* The thought is delicious. A classmate steps in beside me. We smile at each other. We both feel the same. It is communal warmth. I clamber back up the stairs towards the mulled noise at the top. I sway and touch shoulders with people as I make my way back to my seat. I feel warm. I see that the drinks are beyond the halfway point. 'Another round?' 'Aye'. *I've done it*. I walk through the throng and stand behind other people at the bar. The edge is off me. A gap appears at the bar and I slide in. 'Five pints of Stout please'. I hand over the money. My head is hanging down. My muscles are relaxed. I examine the patterns of spilt drink on the bar counter top. My drinks appear into my view. I hand over the money. 'Thank You'. I carry three down at first and then come back for the other two. I lay them down in front of my flat mates and sit down. *I have done it*. I am not thinking I am only feeling and the feeling is warm. I can see that when my turn comes around again I will be on my ninth pint. This sends a warm sensation up my spine.

We leave the bar for another bar. A different consciousness opens up for me. I feel I am in a free open space with no jagged edges. I am floating free. For the first time since that very memorable moment when I entered the classroom I do not care. Bad memories float by in soft malleable bubbles which I look at and push at and laugh at. I realize that this is what being drunk means. *My God there's been a solution here all this time even if I get a break from it once a week I can handle it*. We enter a new bar and I walk around like a moving statue of liberty. I stretch out my arms amidst the throng of people like Jesus on the Cross. I am unworried about whose mind my

L4: Watering Hole

image ends up in and what affect that has on their feelings or thoughts. My eyes connect inward to this new consciousness. It is like a balloon expanding inside my head and pushing against my eyes I spin around in a carefree circle. I push my head back and release myself. I move and talk to people. I walk home happy. I sleep a sound sleep. I awake late the next morning. My head is clear. The room is cold. A sudden convulsion grips me. I am meant to be in class. I was meant to see my counselor. Slowly closing spiked ice walls close in on me. A memory of care freeness from the previous night lights me up like the sun coming down into my head. It's like a new consciousness inside my own head. I think about what waits for me today. *Turning up for the land surveying class in a group that the lecturer put me into in which I cannot speak who all look at me funny.* If all it takes is alcohol to put me into a different state of consciousness then I have found a solution. I drop my head back onto the pillow.

I have to poke my head up into the equation that alcohol works best with chat and chat is easier with alcohol. I sit in the presence of others chatting. I can though lift the glass to my mouth and imbibe. I soak up the atmosphere.

Again we gather around a table in a bar. The drinks begin to flow. Glasses upturn into mouths. Chat is happening. Empty glasses began to pile up on the table. Creamy circles descend down the glasses. I sit in the corner beside the window. I have been quiet for the whole of the session so far. I can manage a few words when spoken to. I have managed to buy a round. I went up without asking. I feel

Persona Medusa

warm. Nobody is passing comment on the fact that I'm not speaking. I slowly move my head and look outside the window onto the street. The sky is caught between light and dark. The buildings are dark silhouettes against the sky. The traffic looks like a Christmas tree. People walk by huddled against the cold. I slowly bring my head back inwards and look at my flat-mates around the table. The table is covered with empty glasses. People in every corner of the bar are full of good spirits. The music is loud and people are dancing. A warm feeling rises up in me. There is a pint of stout in the middle of the table that nobody seems to be drinking. 'Is anyone drinking that?' 'Nah DJ, that's been sat there a while'. I reach out and slide it over to myself. I bend over my pint glass like the rising sun. I grab hold of it between my back teeth. I follow where my feelings lead me and rise with the glass clenched between my teeth upwards. I bend my head backwards. The drink flows into my mouth and down over my chest. I rise my arms up and punch the air. A roar goes up. I sit back down the same way I came up. My clothes are wet and my glass is empty. Images from the past come up and I dance with them. Images from the future come up and I dance with them. We rise up off our seats and start dancing around the table. We lock arms and form a circle and kick out our legs. I fall to the floor. A bouncer grabs me by the arms and starts dragging me towards the door. My flat-mates grab me by the feet. I am suspended in the midair. All I can see is the ceiling. The bouncer turns our whole group around and charges us towards the emergency exit side door of the bar. We bang against the door and the

◼ L4: Watering Hole

door opens. We scatter fall on the footpath outside. We brush ourselves off and stand up. The bouncer is standing in the door with the leg of a stool in his hand. He is batting it against his other hand. We make some mock charges at the bouncer. We laugh and move off home.

● L5: Hunter

I am at a party in another flat. A joint is being passed around and puffed upon. Beers from tins are being swallowed. Cards from stoned hands are being dealt. Eyes pass from one corner to another. A light hangs over all in the smoky air. I see all this from my vantage point in a down and out armchair. The ease at which people do all the things necessary amazes me. They joke. They talk. They laugh. They smoke. They drink. I raise my tin of beer to my mouth and drink. I feel it go all the way down. I take another drink. I watch the joint as it's passed around. There is the card table. There is a haphazard row of seats viewing the game. There am I behind this row. I want the joint to try the joint. I don't want the joint because I will have to take the joint and then pass the joint. I might have to say something like thanks and here. I don't have an ashtray. My tin of beer is empty. I put it down on the floor at the foot of my chair. It joins a steadily increasing circle of empty beer tins. The joint is held in the air before me. I reach out and take it 'Cheers'. I pull on it. I look around for someone to pass it to. I'm surprised it's found its way to me to begin with. I am forced to exert my existence. I get up off my seat and hold the joint close to the next fellows face hoping that he'll see me and I won't have to speak 'Tah'. I slip back down into my seat and take another drink. There is a burgeoning feeling in my groin. I need the toilet. I hold it in as long as possible. My thought does not outweigh nature. I must go or piss myself on the chair. I have pissed myself many times before because I

◆L5: Hunter

could not move. Now I'm nearly paralytic but becoming un-paralyzed. The imagining of pissing my-self on the chair is too much to bear. I picture my-self going to the toilet and then follow the image. I slowly uproot myself. I step over my tin can fairy ring. It feels good to move. I sway and heavy step my way to the toilet. I feel higher than usual. I hover above the toilet and release. *This is progress if I was in the school classroom I'd be wet in my seat by now.* I feel more a part of proceedings now that I've moved from my seat for the first time. I take another drag off the joint and pass it on. I take another drink. I feel like I am floating down into a lovely cool dark well inside my body. I let my brain carry on its processing information and delegation duties while I take a break. I languish on a hammock between two palm trees. The card game is over. People are getting up and putting on their jackets to leave. Others are disappearing out the door and to bed. I keep sitting and stilling. I would have left earlier but could not speak to denounce my departure. I am a paranoid poltergeist afraid to make any sound in case I might be noticed. How can I announce a goodbye when all I have managed to say before that is 'hello', 'here' and 'cheers'? My flat mate turns to me, 'Are you coming?' I place both hands on the arm rest and raise myself from my armchair. I step over the top of my tin can wall and out into the space of the room. My movement is lost in the general moving about. I have been given permission to move. I mumble a goodbye and take off with my flat mate down the street.

Persona Medusa

My feet felt like rubber. I feel like the street is moving towards me not me moving forwards in the street. I am still on my hammock between my two psalm trees. A slight film of wet reflects the street lights from above. Car lights approach and pass. Window lights approach and pass. I look down the length of the street. All the lights make it look like a Christmas tree.

We arrive back at our flat. I see a most beautiful sight, the bed. I flop down and cover myself with a sheet. *I wish I had more than a sheet.* A streetlight's light floods the room. The white blind covering the sash window is lit up like a passageway to somewhere else. I drift into sleep with the image of a white rectangular dazzling door in my head. From my desert island hammock I see the streetlight lit up blind and I must find out what's on the other side.

I brush aside my sheet. I put my feet onto the floor and slowly take in the room. It is small, four walls and a big window. My flat mate is lying asleep on his blowup bed. *Good I won't have to announce my exit to anyone.* I pull back the blind and step behind it. I reach out my hands towards the incoming light. They hit glass. I caress the glass. I take hold of the window and pull it up. The snores from my flat mate seem to be coming from long away but when I look he is still where he was. I push up the window as far as it can go. I clamber out onto the window sill and crouch there. The streetlights lead towards a tree at a junction and further up a hill where they stop. *What is up there?* I drop one leg into the free space of the cold night air and let it swing there. I drop the other foot. I try to feel the ground with

◆**L5**: Hunter

my feet. I slide to the far right of the sill away from the basement drop and the pointed railings. The ground looks closer here. I feel the roughness of the granite sill under my fingers. I see little pieces of quartz glittering. I sit with my bare feet dangling over the edge. A soft drizzle of rain falls from the sky. The houses opposite me look like shielded and helmeted warriors holding their torches in the dark. I look up and down the streetscape and see no one out for a walk. My fingers touch the edge of the sill. I transfer my weight onto my palms. I slip my buttocks off while pressing down on my psalms. I am not expecting the fast fall. I hit the wet ground. I scream in pain and shock. I crumple.

My eyes are at normal level once again. I walk along the street. The crouched house warriors provide a line of direction for me. Small drizzly drops of rain catch light as they fall. I am on my desert island swinging in my hammock. My feet slap the wet pavement. My left foot is limp from the fall. The pain gets me and knocks me out of my hammock. A group of people are hanging around the corner in front of me. I clench my fists. I growl. I climb back into my hammock. When I look up they are gone. *Where'd they go?* I look around. *Where am I?* A police car crawls down the road on the other side to where I walk. *Somebody's in trouble tonight I wonder who they're looking for.* I study the two Gardai as the squad car passes. They seem as much interested in me as I am in them. I turn back to my lit up direction and flop back down in my hammock. 'Excuse me Sir, Could we have a quick word'. I fall out of my hammock. I look to my right.

Persona Medusa

There is a guard there looking at me through the open window of his car. 'Yeah, sure'. The two guards emerge from their car. The headlights shine a beam up the road catching the falling rain. 'It's a nice night for a walk'. I look around. 'Yes it is'. *Who are they looking for?* 'Where are you going?' I look up and down the street. 'I don't know' 'Where are your clothes?' I look down at myself. I am wearing a white T-shirt and a pair of patterned boxer shorts. 'I don't know'. I scratch my head. My hammock supports have broken and it has hit the ground. 'Where do you live', 'Oh, just down the road there' 'Would you be able to direct us there if we get you in the car' 'Yeah, sure' I'm beginning to feel like I do in that nightmare that I have where I go to school and realize I'm missing my shoes. I bow down and get into the back seat of the car. *Do this with dignity.* The warmth feels welcoming. I look intently out the window. I don't want to appear stupid by not being able to direct them to where I live. I spot my house. 'That's the one'. *Thank God* 'Are you sure?' 'Yeah'. The two guards accompany me up-to the front door. I lift up my hand and ring the door bell. *Please someone answer.* The door opens. My flat mate stands there. 'Do you know this fellow? Does he live here?' 'Yes. What happened?' 'Oh, we found him wondering up the street on his own' The Guards are laughing. I feel relief. I enter the house and follow my flat mate up the stairs. He is now laughing. I am liberated. There is my beautiful bed. I clamber on to it and ly down. My flat mate puts his head down too. I can feel sleep creeping up on me again. I can see the lit up blind there drawing me to it. I sit up and start to put

◆L5: Hunter

on my jeans. My flat mate awakes 'What are you doing? What are you putting on your jeans for?' 'In case I jump out the window again, I want to be well dressed'. I decide to get up and watch TV for the rest of the night, just in case.

The morning has arrived. Bright winter light shines through the window. I have a throbbing pain in my leg. I can't make it into class today. I am glad for that. *What was I looking for last night?*

▲ S1: Zombie

A mystery tour has been organized by the student union in college. There are rumors that it is a bus trip to a night club. I am invited along by two of my flat-mates. I accept and look forward to the point when I lose my self. We are to meet in the student bar for a drink and then board the bus.

They are there as they said they would be behind two glasses of white topped black. I catch their eyes and nod my head they do likewise. 'Would you like another?' 'Ah, sure one for the road'

We sit and drink. They show me that they have each a half bottle of whiskey wrapped in a brown paper bag at their feet. I must get likewise. I have a quick imagining of what it would be like at the bottom of that bottle.

We leave the pub and out into the cool fresh air. The aftertaste of the Stout caresses my palate and intensifies when it connects with the fresh air. I get myself a half bottle of whiskey.

The bus pulls up and I feel the same feelings as always rise up again. This time though I have a weapon in my brown paper bag. Soon I won't care. It is like a safety valve to open a trapdoor in my head.

The bus comes. *Speak. Speak. Speak.* The two lads sit together and I sit on the seat in front of them. *At least that's that bit over.* The seats are comfy. I can't see over the top of the seat in front of me and

♠S1: Zombie

people behind me can't see over the top at me and I am there with my bottle. I have never drunk whiskey neat or this quantity of it before.

I raise the whiskey bottle to my mouth and imbibe. It causes a fire in my throat. I swallow. It feels warm. I watch the city then the countryside passing by the window. My bottle is gone in the first hour. I sink into the chair. I can hear the two lads behind me and the rest of the people on the bus. A face appears over my seat like the rising sun with a big smile spread across it. I smile back. 'Are you not indulging?' I roll the brown paper bag over my bottle revealing its emptiness. He laughs.

A warm geyser fountains over my body. I look out the window and back at the people sitting across from me. I lean the side of my head against the seat and feel like I'm falling down into a deep dark well. I look out from the bottom of this body well. I am lord here.

The bus comes to a halt. People are getting up and leaving. My two flat-mates rise behind me and exit their seats. I sit and wonder what to do. They tap me on the shoulder and I follow.

By the time my foot touches the ground outside of the bus I don't know where I am or who I am.

We enter a night club. We fall about the place drunk. I stand at a high table with a pint in front of me. Somebody waves their hands in front of my face. I see it but I am too far below to care. I take another look at the drink in front of me and realize that I've had enough, maybe more than enough. I walk to the door with the bright exit sign above it.

Persona Medusa

I have no idea where I am. The roads are lit up to a point and then enter into countryside. To look for the bus doesn't enter my head. *Walk.* I walk up one of the roads and keep walking. I reach the point where the lights stop and I continue into the dark. I veer off the beaten track and take moonlit shortcuts through fields of silvery slivery grass. I slip and trip in the mud as cows look on. I come back to consciousness intermittently and take in the surroundings and disappear again. I come too after walking a further distance. I look out again. The same scene hits me. I disappear and come up. My mind starts playing tricks on me. It tells me that home is just around the next corner and so I keep walking. *I have to be home in time for work or I am going to lose my job or worse have to explain why I am late.*

A slow blinding light lights up the country road from behind me. I step into the grass verge and turn around. I don't want to be a black and white road accident statistic. The car stops. *I hope he's not going to ask me for directions.* My hand automatically comes up to shield my eyes from the light. There's a figure behind the driving wheel. He sits still. *Turn around and continue on your way this guy could be a weirdo.* The car door opens and a foot comes out followed by the rest of the man. 'Excuse me, are you all right?' 'Yeah, fine' 'You look a bit lost. Do you know where you are?', 'Yeah. I'm just outside Mullingar. My home is just around the corner' 'No, you're in Navan. Mullingar is 60 km away' 'What? I'm sure I live just around the corner. These bushes look familiar' 'No. You're in the wrong county altogether. You're not on the run from the law, are you?' 'No, I'm on

◆S1: Zombie

a mystery tour from college' 'All right then. Get in the car and I'll ring the guards and see what they'll want to do with you?'

I climb in to his car and we move off with his headlights lighting the way. It's a lovely little cocoon away from the dark and the cold and the muck and the animals. His headlights fall up on a country pub. He drives up to it and parks in front. 'Come on in here. I'll make a phone call'. I follow him in and stand in the middle of the deserted, gone closing time bar. I sway from left and right and backwards and forwards. The bartender looks on. I don't detect a very pleased look on his face. 'Get him out of here. I'll lose my license' 'Come on Jim just let us use the phone' 'No, get out'.

We pull away from the country pub and head down the road. The beams of the car light up the eerie bushes. A rabbit flits across the road. We pull into the man's driveway. The two of us trudge through the gravel driveway towards his front door. I see concern in the man's face. He silently opens the door. 'Come on in, step into the kitchen. He calls for his wife to come down. She descends the stairs. 'Who are you?' 'I'm DJ' 'He's lost. I found him drunk on the side of the road after falling out of a ditch' 'Oh, my God, and look at the state of you. You're covered head to toe in grass and earth. What have you been up to?' 'I don't know? I was sitting on a bus, I was walking on a road' 'Here, I normally use this for brushing the dog, but now, stand there now' 'Thanks'

I stand in the kitchen. I feel as if a plug has been removed from my mouth. There is no gap between the thoughts of my mind and the utterances from my mouth. It is as if my mind and voice are one. I think and speak. What I speak is nonsense but it's better than nothing.

The man hands me the phone. 'It's your mother on the line' 'Hello' 'Where are you?' 'This man tells me I'm in Navan' 'Do you want us to come and get you?' 'No I'll leave in the morning' 'The guards told us you were found delirious wandering the roads in Meath. Are you okay?' 'Yeah I'm fine, just a bit too much to drink'

The man's wife has laid out some blankets on the couch. 'You just go to sleep on the couch there. Tomorrow is another day. We'll see how you feel then. That's normally where the dog sleeps but you can have it for tonight'. I lay down and fall down into sleep.

It is morning. I awake smelly breathed, shaggy, dirty and with a bouncing headache. I roll over and notice the dog looking inquisitively at me probably wondering who is sleeping in his bed.

◆ S2: Attack

I put on my walkman and headphones and leave the college building into the cold night. Street lights light the way. My warm breath enters the cold air. People pass me by huddled down. I walk up the side street and around the front of the College. I head on my way to my digs. The surrounds get steadily more derelict as I progress. Suddenly I seem to be the only person on the street. I can feel the freeze feeling switching on. I walk onward. This feels different to the other times when I was in the class room and felt threatened. It is as if on some level of consciousness I knew I was not under threat there. Now as I look at the dark and the buildings and the absence of people out in the cold a long way from home and family that slim conscious relief is taken away. I imagine the end of the journey, a warm house and cup of tea.

A man appears from behind the corner and approaches me. 'Would you like this naggin of whiskey? I don't need it anymore'. *I'm trying to change and I should be open to new experiences.* 'Ok'. I put a puzzled look on my face as if I'm a connoisseur of fine whiskey and am wondering why anyone in their right mind would want to give up a naggin of whiskey. An image of my Dad standing in the nice warm kitchen pouring some Jameson into a glass comes into my mind. He walks away from me and I walk on. I feel cold. I know the encounter is not finished. I can feel him looking at me but I do not turn around. I decide to consciously speed up my walk but not enough that he might notice. He's beside me again. 'Would you like to go for a drink?' 'Nah. Sorry. I have to get home'. He continues to walk beside me. I feel cold. There are people around. They walk swiftly with hunched shoulders and bowed heads. In better circumstances I could not even ask for help. There's a corner coming up in front of me. I continue to walk and look straight ahead hoping that the guy walking beside me leaves me alone. *Why is he still there?* He charges into me and grabs me by the arm. 'Don't scream or do anything stupid. You'll come up this alleyway with me and around the corner at the top. I've got hepatitis B. You don't want to lose your life over something as silly as this?' I look down and see the syringe held against my arm. I feel cold. Pictures of newspapers flash in my minds eye of when I was safe and warm and reading of reports of muggings in Dublin that happened to other people. *Sure it was only a matter of time before this happened to me why wouldn't it happen to me this will make a great story to tell to people who will I tell it to I don't have anyone to speak to this is a real situation I better concentrate on getting out of it or I won't get a chance to find someone to tell it to or I'll live and it will be a story with an unhappy ending he hasn't asked for money so what does he want with me around the top corner this is not good.* The man has his head down and is ploughing forward he has a compact rugby players build. I move as slowly as possible. 'Come up this alleyway with me and around the corner at the top'. I see the corner at the top and decide that if I go around that corner with him I am finished. My mind makes a decision which there is no questioning with. *No matter*

♠S2: Attack

what if I get a chance to escape no matter how small I will take it. The man does not know I've made a decision but it warms me. I feel my life is on the line. All thoughts of everything else disappear. I start to shout at the man. 'Do you want money?' I push my hand into my pocket and produce my wallet. I move it in front of his face. 'Take my wallet you bollix!' 'Take my fucking wallet you fucker!' I open it in front of his face so he can see the two wings and the one paper money protruding out. 'Take it! Take it! Take it! You fuck!' I cannot stop shouting. 'How much is in it?' 'I don't know, have a look'. His right hand still grips me on my wrist holding me against my will. He reaches up for my wallet with his syringe wielding left hand. I take note that the syringe is now away from my wrist. He grabs my wallet with his syringe hand and holds it up to his eyes to examine its contents. I see that his concentration is broke. The syringe is far enough away from my wrist for me to attempt a maneuver. *This is my chance.* I simultaneously start to turn and reach across with my right arm. I grab my wallet in mid turn and pull it away from the man's grip. 'Yoink!' The turn breaks the grip he has on my left wrist. I am facing towards the side street and I start to run. 'Come back here!' 'Fuck you!' *Why would I go back to you you stupid cunt.* The cobblestones are wet. *Don't fall.* I imagine the skirmish on the ground and the man bearing over me. *Please God if you're up there I will give up smoking if you leave me with enough breath to outrun this guy.* I concentrate on each step of my run. I reach the side street. I turn to my right carefully. I continue to run up towards the main street. I see car lights passing by the mouth of the street. I see people and shops. *Someone will help someone will notice.* I run towards these lights. The man is still giving chase. 'Come back here', 'Fuck off, fuck off, fuck off'. My walkman falls off and bangs against the ground. 'Fuuuuuck!' I had saved up a lot of cereal tokens for that. I reach the main street and take a right turn. My flat is just up the road. I dart across into the middle of the road. I want to draw as much attention as possible on myself. I run down along the white line. I see people turning their heads. That's what I want. Cars slow down. 'Don't get involved'. I look back. The man has given up the chase. He has stopped. He looks to be bent over and panting for breath. 'Fucker!' I turn and walk up the road. I'm shaking. I feel tall. I see people looking at me. not because I'm not saying anything but because I've been shouting and moving. I feel warm. I remember my walkman that fell off my belt while being chased. I take a few steps towards the man. 'Fucker!' People hurry past. I turn towards my flat. I feel cold with the thought that he might get his breath back and chase after me again. Nobody here would help me. I quicken my pace and head for home. I realize I'm still carrying the naggin of whiskey. I place it down at a bus stop.

 I arrive in the door. My dig mate is watching TV and chatting to the digs mother. 'Hi'. My body is shaking. I sit down at the end of the table and listen to their chatting hoping for an opening that I can jump into. The opening doesn't come. I'm being quiet for too long again. The longer quiet the harder it is to break out. Dinner arrives and with

♠ S2: Attack

the clatter of plates and cling of cutlery I speak. 'Thanks, looks nice'. I congratulate myself on the looks nice. I keep the attack to my-self.

I move my change around in my pocket as I wait for the bus to take me to my digs. My bags with too much stuff are beside me on the footpath in the shelter of a shop front. My back is against the metal shutters. I see two lads in fastened around the waist anoraks walking up the path. They have stubble above their lips. I turn away as soon as I see them. They have seen me too but they don't turn away. They pass me by. I breathe a sigh of relief. *Don't turn your head to follow them.* I look across the road. There are lots of people around. I look at my bag lying at my feet. *What will I do if they rob that how would I explain that maybe they haven't seen my bag.* I push it behind my feet. They enter into my eye sight once again. *This isn't good.* My blood has turned to sugar. They pass me by and then stop a few feet away. They whisper to each other. I see a smile on one of their faces. They make a beeline towards me. Both of them stand in front of me. 'Hey Bud. Don't scream. I have a knife in my pocket. Hand over your money'. I think about lashing out and hitting but my body does the opposite. It pummels me inward. 'All I have is my bus fare' 'Give it here'. They walk off laughing. I look around. Everyone is going about their business and nobody has noticed. I pick up my overfull bags and start to walk. My heart is thumping. I think I am being vigilant for more assailants but I seem to be dropping into and out of consciousness. If anyone does make a move there is not much I can do. I feel cold. I walk past shop units with apartments on top. *They look safe.* I

Persona Medusa

pass the mouth of the street of my previous attack. I feel cold. I arrive at the door of my digs. I enter and close the door behind me. There is no one else here. I breathe a sigh of relief. I make tea and toast. I go to bed and feel the dark like it is the inside of a predator's mouth. Closed and chewing.

I leave my flat on a cold winters evening in search of a blanket to keep me warm at night. I pace the flat trying to pick up the courage to go out and into the unpredictability of the city. S*urely it couldn't happen again. I cannot stay here forever anyways.* I go for the door, open, close, stand back, breath in and out. The evening is crisp and fresh. I feel alive. A couple passes by. I close the door behind me. I shove my hands into my pockets, bow my head and walk briskly up the street. Lights of seasonal festivity catch my eye. *Must get a blanket so I can sleep in warmth.* I walk into the city center. I feel warm amongst the general milling of people. The anonymity of the busy city provides a relief to me. It's unlikely I will face a familiar face coming towards me and if I do there are lots of shields around. I walk into the shop. I buzz as I see a blanket that I want. I imagine having a warm night's sleep. I hand over the money. *Great!*

I turn and head back in the direction I came. I leave the busy center behind. Gradually the people get fewer. I begin to feel the freeze feeling once again. My pace quickens. I can now see only a couple of people. I turn the corner to the street where my flat is on. Out of the corner of my eye I catch sight of a group of lads huddled together in an alleyway just off the street. I see them clock me as I walk by. I can

◆ S2: Attack

see their thoughts expressed on their faces. *There's a weak one lets attack him.* Two of the lads give their friends a nod and a pat and break away from the group. I hope they are just going home. I feel they are not. They appear beside me. Both of them are on my right side. The nearest fellow turns his face to me. 'I've got a screwdriver in my pocket, do as I say and you won't get hurt'. The freeze feeling has come but I keep walking. My front door is just a few steps away. *At least it's not a syringe or a knife this time and at least these fellows are better dressed.* I say nothing for the first few seconds. I reach my house and make to turn into it. The fellow beside me gets impatient at my non recognition of his threat. He lays his hand on my shoulder. 'I'm serious. I've got a screwdriver. I'll stick ya if you don't hand over your money'. *I'm so close to my home.* 'Give me your money!' I feel cold. I imagine being stuck with a screwdriver and weigh this against the prospect of handing over my money. I feel my hand and arm by my side. I move my fingers unseen. An image of physically striking this person enters my head. The movements required to carry this out are too many. He would see it coming. Even if it did connect it would be like a drooping flower against his cheek. It would not be cinematic. I lift out my wallet from within my pocket. I open it and display it to the fellows face. There is not a penny inside. 'I don't have any money, see'. He takes my wallet to investigate. He spreads its wings. He looks inside like a vulture pecking himself. Nothing. The two lads look at me. They hand the wallet back to me. 'There', 'Sorry about that'. They stride on up the street. I shudder. I walk in-

Persona Medusa

side and close and lock the door behind me. Nobody is here. I walk up and down the room. I try to relax. I watch some TV. I check to make sure there is no-one in the flat. 'Fuck You!' I stamp the floor. I advance towards the kettle. I boil some water and make a cup of tea. I stand sipping the tea. My hand is shaking. I console myself. *When I'm auld sitting wherever the test of still being alive and having enjoyed will be silent pontification over a cup of tea this is just another of them things.*

◆ S3: Death Roll

That familiar surrender to sleep is upon me. I feel something else there too. It begins gently, like a fish nibbling at my toes, flows quickly, unstoppably up through my legs, pelvis, abdomen, chest, arms and head. It is like I am being slowly submerged into ice water. The gently nibbling fish turns into a toothless shark who pulls me irresistibly under. I try to wake myself up and get back to the surface but its grip gets tighter. The icy water encloses over my head. I am deep inside and cannot break free. I do not even know which way is up or down. It whips and tosses me about in nightmare dark. I hear footsteps striking the wooden corridor floor outside my closed door, feint at first, then getting louder and louder, faster and faster. They stop. I open my eyes. People with familiar faces stand at the edge of my bed. They smile. *What are they doing here?* Their smiles turn into grimaces. They wield bats and sticks in their hands. They raise their weapons above their heads and swing them down upon me in a cascade of strikes. I twist and thrash trying to escape. I try to catch the weapons in my hands but they smash my hands. I try to scream. I try to shout 'Fuck off'. No noise comes. Any noise at all would break the nightmare. The black depth has pressurized my voice into my body. I thrash and thrash like a fish on a boat. I sense the final blow. I let go. My feet spring up lifting me and my duvet off the bed. I am awake panting for breath in still darkness.

Persona Medusa

I stare at the ceiling. The feeling is still there nibbling at my toes. *Stay awake don't let that happen again get up and turn on the light.* It's too late. It grabs me again and pulls me under. My new roommate stands over me. He smiles at first. W*hat's he doing at the side of my bed?* His smile changes to a grimace. He grabs me by the throat. He twists me around to upside down on the bed. Drags me across the bed, onto the floor, across the floor, up the wall, pins me there, then up and across the ceiling and down the other wall. I punch and choke in the bed. I feel death coming. I let go. I gasp and pant again.

I sit up awake now. I stare at the corner of the ceiling where the walls meet there. I am sling shot forward towards that point. I feel like I am going somewhere where there is no return from. The journey to the origin point is taking for ever even though I am travelling at speed. *Is the room moving towards me or am I moving towards the room.* The point gets closer and closer. I let go. I wake up lying on my bed. I don't remember falling asleep. *I thought I said not to fall asleep.*

There is a something at the foot of my bed. I do not know what it is. I can feel menace off it. My hairs stand on end. I can feel a fuzzy cold engulf me. It stares and stares. I stare and stare. *This can't be real*. It stays longer in my vision than my rational mind can take. *It is real*. I let go. It dissipates in front of me and I am left staring into space.

My head collapses onto the pillow. I shakily, weakly go to the light switch. I turn on the light and leave it on.

◆ S4: Blood Trail

How do I copy and paste in this program I don't know must ask don't let anyone know I don't know not yet keep looking at computer screen I have to ask speak speak speak try and do it myself this doesn't make sense speak speak speak.....

Oh no my computers crashed I've lost all my work for the day make a noise say fuck or shit or something anything speak speak speak.....

Come on I haven't spoken to anyone else in the building all day only a good morning without names to the people in my room go down the stairs and into my colleagues rooms and have a chat just roam around shooting the breeze the receptionist doesn't even know I'm here go on down and chat with her flirt even come on I can do it why should I have to think these things come on stop looking at your computer move your ass speak speak speak.....

Drinnnnng Drinnnnng *answer it it's your job who's on the other end what are they going to say what am I going to say have I screwed up calm down* Drinnnng Drinnnng. 'Hello......'

Where's my job on the list there no 10 I'll have to say something then how's the job going relax relax refuse tea my hands are shaking hide them under the table my feet are shaking keep them under the table speak to the person I'm next to release some tension everyone else is so polished this is just second nature to these people swallow

Persona Medusa

calm down please calm down listen to me please it's nearly your turn speak speak speak.....

'Drinks on Friday People!' *No No No how do I get out of this come on go for it I've drank before this can't work tell him no then just say no then they'll think I'm weird no just go pretend I'm excited like everyone else I read lots of people feel the way I do I don't see that speak speak speak.....*

I hate this bit voices there all getting ready for the night out just sit here in this empty room until it all dies down then follow them out at the end if no one knows I'm in here nobody will be thinking it's weird that I'm in here by myself wait they're moving towards the door how are they able to shout and voice so easily go go go go is that the door is that the alarm being set is that the key turning It's too late wait wait ok leave there goes the alarm go home nobody knows it's me there's always next Friday for social drinks.....

Say something say something stop thinking to say something and say something I'll have to buy a round of drinks shortly how can I say anything they're talk is moving so fast and laughter so much laughter at least join in the laughter that I can do 'Ha Ha Ha Huh Huh Huh' *at least they might know I'm here now* 'Hey, He who speaks a lot would you like a drink?' 'Yeah sure'.....

The Christmas party is coming up I need to get out of here before that I should go travelling maybe I'll come back different find myself as they say postpone my start in my profession will I speak when travelling though I don't know it's not likely to be any different I have

S4: Blood Trail

enough money to do it I should keep my money will I last in a job when I come back will I get a job abroad…..

My numbers coming up next forty three should have come earlier there would be less people think about something else it's only at number 30 that's thirteen people in front of me that's thirteen people before I have to speak that book said to fidget if I get nervous to use up energy breath yeah deep breaths in out in out in out 'Hi, I'd like a multi-stop ticket please, Bangkok, Sydney, Los Angeles, New York, Dublin'*…..*

What am I doing here this place is so shiny what business have I to be getting on a plane because I have a few quid in my pocket what would the makers of the plane think there's security I don't see anyone I know good nobody really speaking here good take off my belt and shoes everyone else is doing it I should have dumped all this change stop hopping ouch bloody belt that never happened before don't go red keep calm I've paid to be here nobody here knows me shoes on belt on don't sweat so much none of these other people look as perturbed as I keep your head high don't slouch be aware of everything I've got eyes in the back of your head now walk I've made it nice shops I have a purpose here I don't have to walk in circles there is no one to avoid wait I'm missing something my bag no no no stay calm back to security there it is 'Thanks' 'You really should be more careful'*…..*

Do I try to make conversation with the person beside me come on I'm on an adventure once in a life time who am I kidding watch the *movie stay calm which dinner chicken beef come on make sure she hears me first time stay calm I'm nex*t 'Chicken please'…..

We're down clap much appreciated here we go people are saying goodbye to the air hosts at the top calm down breathe it looks very humid out there hope them bags don't fall on me only twenty people in front of me do any of them feel the same why how can I remember if I can't forget 'Thank You' *nice smiles I'm free again…..*

I thought Bangkok would be sunny it's so humid and wet there's the taxi rank there's the buses too much having to speak in the bus rooting for change have a cigarette that sucked now my breath smells have another the further away I keep from social interaction the less embarrassment I'll receive I'll take the taxi I'm not even sure where I'm staying the adventure begins now who am I kidding forget the past I've already remembered to think this 'Can you take me to a good hostel please'…..

Foods nice is she a he she be careful too many don't want to get in any trouble don't make eye contact she's coming towards me 'Would you like some fun' 'No thanks' *why not what have I to lose what am I afraid of Jesus Christ* 'You should go some-place else' *nod it's wet out here the air is warm what's that a tap on my shoulder somebody going to rape and murder me,* 'Sorry, this money fell out of your pocket' 'Oh thanks very much' *well done on the very much this place seems all right don't expect to see anyone I know around the next corner great will not have to say or not say hi to anyone…..*

◀ S4: Blood Trail

There's a tuk tuk will I get no too much rooting for change agreeing a price having to speak easier to walk no matter how far Khao San Rd that's where I want to be the beach nice t shirts nice bars and restaurants don't make stop too long someone might speak to me keep walking this is the end turn around and walk back go in somewhere nice restaurants pick one which has the fewest people don't want to be left without a seat walking drifting in open space with a plate in my hands trying to look comfortable and feeling the opposite this is the end of the other end this time stop in somewhere or I'm going to starve to death in there all right the next one maybe now in the next in go in plenty of seats here sit down take a menu 'chicken and rice and big beer please' *immense pride well done look at all them people passing by sheet rain thunder claps stuck at the wall can't move can't sit down look at me now nice beer glass getting empty have to ask for more ignore that feeling the beer will take care of it just keep going getting closer to the bottom try to catch waiters eye* 'Another beer please' *receipts on a spear nice another another what do I do when I need to go to the toilet must go take bag with me will my seat be there when I get back don't care ah ha* 'Guten-tag' 'How's it going?' 'Where are you from?' 'Ireland' 'Ah yes Ireland' 'What's the temperature like there?' 'Eh, not great' *please don't ask me anything about my home town or friends or girl friends or football must leave now* 'got to go' *Jesus watch it splash jump there's a tuk tuk fuck it in* 'Back to hostel' *wait a minute my bag ah Jesus Christ not again for fuck sake run* 'Thanks' 'You really should be more careful'.....

Persona Medusa

This is a nice bar dark and cool just the way I like it I should go over there and play pool with them people put money on the table who am I kidding up-tip that drink take it easy I should be out there having fun I should be talking to people will this beer make me do that wall is there no one I can talk to about my experiences who'd understand come on tah fuck get up and do something speak speak speak my glass is getting empty again that music is loud kind of good though like they're having great fun over there shit I'm getting too self conscious here now I'm feeling too awkward to get off my chair and make it over to the toilets come on alcohol knock down thoughts knock down memories take over let feeling flow has self consciousness taken me over completely the bloody alcohol seems to be going to my thoughts getting them drunk and them running riot in my head.....

What a huge train station what am I doing here so many people there's the ticket kiosk ten or so people in front right lots of people she looks nice 'One to Surat Thani, please' brilliant tickets in hand a twelve hour train journey there may not be much expectation to speak or to have fun there's beds on the train I can sleep I don't have to talk to any-one just board hopefully the sound of the tracks will lull me to sleep maybe a few beers I had beers before on a train they were nice.....

No-one else seems to be drinking don't be the first don't want to look crazy or anything or worse still give the impression that I'm a party mad fellow people will expect me to have lots to say here comes the waiter keep attentive hear him make sure he hears me then imbibe

S4: Blood Trail

to survive 'Chicken and rice please' *come on the night so I can just lay down in bed with the curtains pulled that Thai waiter has a Hurley stick in his hand there must be some Irish on this carriage I should get up and walk up and down and talk to them go on go on go on speak speak get up up up up by one what if its someone I know do I know anyone they'd know it's possible there's laughter and the sound of cans opening definitely Irish go over what's the point in travelling if I don't that bloody feeling again ignore it come on now I feel sick it was a good idea to bring nothing that could identify me no football shirt hurleys or anything like that there goes the sliotar its getting dark wish I had someone to talk to that's ridiculous that's what people say when to sit beside me not me when I sit beside others or on my own* 'Excuse me Sir, we have to make the beds' ' Ok' *it's great here like my own private room for the first time in a long time just for a six or so hours though nice curtains what's going to happen when I get there I've only really spoken to people when I've had a request for information or food or tickets so far what about just saying something out there and see if anyone picks up on it out there is still a strange place nice underside of bunk Thailand countryside I will do this, it will be good what's that a hand* 'Hey' 'Sorry' *sleep come on stop thinking.....*

   That was a terrible sleep like my eyes were awake but my brain was asleep bright hazy morning dense jungle greenery waving washerwomen men with tools watch so long hello beach is this Surat Thani I wonder ask someone go on 'Yeah Surat Thani' *that's grand don't*

Persona Medusa

need to ask have overheard someone else asking and someone else answer that's great I'm very aware of what's going on eyes and ears in the back of my head why can't I speak just naturally though.....

I'm hungry there's a tuck shop there's plenty of seats go on it's going to be awkward rooting in my pocket for money it's either that or starve I should have brought something there's a coke in the fridge I can pick that up myself I won't have to ask anyone and a prepackaged sandwich sorted the price is on there great I have the money sorted in my hand 'Thanks' I do love smiles these plastic picnic type red and white tables remind me of home why does it make me feel good bright stickers all around where's mine there's the fella giving them out please 'Thanks' whose going to the same island as I should I try to speak to them stop kidding.....

Don't fall in you never know what's under water very green where to go now something to lean against at least I'm not part of a group that will disperse or get into groups where ever I go there I am lean against these metal railings relax go on the sun is out your in Thailand there's lots of beautiful people around this is taking a long time I thought the crossing would be quick my back is getting sore against the railings I should move somewhere else where no I have a spot here walk around no stay my back move stay in the same spot and stretch all now back can't be too much longer there's the v of the front slicing through the Gulf of Thailand and look there's the wake disappearing at the back why don't I talk to someone come on there it is Koh Pah Ngan' I can get excited now like the other people go on go

◀ S4: Blood Trail

on what's holding me back move turn do more than look something to look at permission to turn while everyone else is turning aaah away from the metal railings keep my hand there though just in case island eyes and minds on everyone.....

There's the pier say we're there to the person beside me hollow sound waves against hull there goes the anchor there go the ropes come on people are beginning to talk more and more I'm looking more and more as the person I'm trying to escape at last across the gangplank don't trip I'll have to say something are they gathering at the other side do I wait with them no keep away from the groups don't pretend I haven't spoken to anyone they're getting taxis to where they're going nobodies hanging around too long good do that too wait let the crowds escape first and then hail a taxi less people will have to see me raise an arm.....

A café go in there's plenty of free tables in there to escape somewhere else find a place to stay yes ok 'Big Beer Please' there Haad Rin beach the most popular place most popular let go have fun go on that's where the full moon party is.....

Hope I get my passport back white sands nice beach hut brilliant more sand than sky wait over the hill the sea on my door step wow brilliant now what to do three weeks here sleep now no meetings no having to talk am I running though nah time out two weeks until full moon party sip a beer think where to go that bar beside the shop what would I do sit by myself I've been out before by myself wait for them to fill up and get loud with music then slip in tomorrow maybe come

Persona Medusa

on do something I can't spend all my time sipping beer on a balcony congratulating myself on having gone to the shop 'Beer and toilet roll please' 'The bare essentials I see' *that's what she said with a smile that was funny that's done now.....*

Book shops clothes shops food shops restaurants bars motor cycle rentals right walk back down the street drop in somewhere where book shop examine some books I'm doing something well done there's trainspotting buy now back.....

Where to lay down lovely white sand soft and warm a massage at every step too close to them too loud too good looking they've got a football there will do a bit away from any communication threat come on why sand ripples aren't very comfortable wriggle and smooth them out no don't someone might be looking see more sky than earth now book all the way to Thailand to read a book okay just a few pages bloody grey mongrel dogs vicious drooling mouths can't they fight somewhere else the sea curvy women colorful sarongs would I even speak to them come on Oh rain I can go now.....

Full moon party today why don't I say something to all them people passing by the balcony it's not time to have your nose stuck in a book I'm not even reading I'm thinking of what I'm not going to do moonlight and neon and fire beach right walk down the beach them glow lights look good thumping music beach bars packed looks like too much work to order at the bar would anyone hear me they're doing everything I wish I could do are they happy though probably I think that Thai lady is coming towards me she's fit why has she got an

◆S4: Blood Trail

umbrella though it's not raining say that to her 'why the umbrella, it's not raining' 'I know' *whys she flicking her eyelashes what does that mean carry on go on wow that was some buzz speaking is great the greatest thing in existence the buzz is unreal I think she was flirting with me I was with her go and get a drink* 'A bucket of Joy, please' *nice what's that feeling is that the drug taking effect lovely can one feeling trump another does feeling trump thought if body came before mind then feeling does trump thought it's been around longer don't be standing straight now go on dance the vibrations of the music feel good drop one knee now the other I'm kind of moving now keep doing it let the music take effect raise your arms in the air maybe later lovely lighted eyes leaving light trail in their wake try to connect who do I think I am I'm the guy who was stuck to the wall in school who never spoke for thirteen years what am I doing dancing on a beach in Thailand these people don't know if I speak to them they will know oh my brain feels electrified it seems to be expanding in my head let go let go keep drinking get another bucket I'll have to release say something to someone anyone go on move hands up in the air good dance yes that feels good now don't make a fool out of yourself them fellows over there are dancing and not speaking to anyone like they're in their own world maybe I could do that twist drop your knees drop your shoulders this isn't abandon too much thinking carry on anyways lighted people their image lasts longer than normal when they move right home now before my head explodes.....*

Persona Medusa

'One jungle safari ticket to Chang Mai please' *why do I always speak from my mouth how do I speak from lower down another train trip get away from the Island I feel like the asshole from the beach who goes to these places and just watches films twelve hours to Bangkok then another twelve up to Chang Mai that's twenty four hours without expectation to have fun or speak what will the jungle tour be like just do it black and white graffiti wall of thought flat this is what was is now is I should I help him make the bed no I'd only get in the way stand back nice green scenery out the window.....*

Back in Bangkok don't leave the train station I mightn't find my way back sit on that bench there and wait for your train shit there's two fellows in Galway county colors they're coming this way 'Hello, I seen you in Haadrin. Are you Irish?', Yeah', 'Thought so, me and my mate are just travelling around, we took pills in Haadrin and stayed up the whole two weeks we were there, we were riding women left right and center, we tried acid and had a great time. How'd you do?' 'Oh yeah same as that' *thank God they're gone relax again what do I mean I'm meant to be travelling to meet people jaysus get back on that train now travel with purpose instead of circling the train has purpose do I.....*

I'm going on a jungle safari me why just because I think I should or I want to I don't know it's not until tomorrow anyways relax here lay on the bed will there be many people on it just speak come on now's your chance.....

❦ S4: Blood Trail

Isn't someone going to say something come on their hardly waiting for me to say something this is one bumpy ride is it more comfortable for someone else to be talking and me to be silent or for everyone to be silent if someone seen us now they would think the whole group a bore say that thing about the bumpy road go on say it 'Rough road' 'Yeah' *there I've said something and got a response and a smile from a sexy English rose no less I've contributed lean back yes see I'm not the quietest one here I've said a sentence more than anyone else who am I kidding I've been here before.....*

Am I seriously hunting for frogs in a jungle in Thailand myself from years ago would never believe this I've come far from the wall now half way across the world the waters cold hope theres no snakes around what's that over there is there crocodiles in this river what's this river even called that German fellow is going awful close to that small drop if he slips and falls over he'll be swallowed up by the dark jungle there there's a frog transfixed in the light frozen am I the predator now feels good there the guides got him breakfast there they are now all laid out on the grill Jesus on the Cross frogs dinner and whiskey why didn't the two German lads or the two English girls bring bottles of whiskey oh well don't forget to speak the crackle of the fire is nice listen to the old hunter tell his tales at least it takes pressure off me these lads like the whiskey should have brought some more 'I once had a monkey in my sights and was about to let go the string when I noticed the monkey was crying. I realized then that monkeys do have souls' *nobody likes to be hunted powerless sip my whiskey*

Persona Medusa

there isn't much left why not ask for more it is yours after all no why didn't they bring bottles why don't I ask.....

The mosquito nets make the beds look like kneeling ghosts waiting to be beheaded I can't wait to sleep under them nets away from social engagement there's not enough whiskey round to forget who I am or am nailed to be the cross to carry lay down now close your eyes in darkness no one can see me now again jungle tour finishes tomorrow that's that I'm nearly there another accomplishment what other accomplishments have I achieved well something to talk about if even.....

'Cheers' 'Cheers' 'Cheers' Cheers' 'Cheers' put your glass between your lips and drink now say something look around is there anything to remark on no just listen to what the others are saying don't kid myself I'm not listening I'm trying to speak but can't am I trying very hard yes the feeling has blasted even my ability to live to gain knowledge of things to develop opinions 'Bye' 'Bye' 'Bye' 'Bye' 'Bye'.....

Hello Sydney Australia this is the start of a new me forget about the previous me that was only yesterday and every day before am I far enough away now for my past to dissipate.....

Lovely city walk around look at things there's Sydney Opera house what to do have a beer take it in walk around come on I can do this in Mullingar do something different go to Bondi beach I'll have to root for change do it nice heavy waves lay down here speak to someone is the day nearly over.....

◆S4: Blood Trail

Oh no did he see me turn away he's a witness rotten banana skin orange peels sandwich crusts no walk into the crowd disappear avoid eye contact at all costs oh no 'Well look who it *is*' 'Hi' *what a timid hi I've lost it now has the past been and gone at all whys he smiling like that he knows* 'Do you remember so and so and so and so' 'Oh Yeah, I wonder where they are now. Are you here for the night?' 'Nah, we're moving on to the late bar across the road' 'Well fuck off there, then' 'You know I remember you in school. I remember you used to shite yourself' *that grin punch him do something ouch my cigarette just do it in his face there you go you fucker* 'Fucker' *all this way and here I am back where I started the same feelings come up and get me channels to the past* 'And don't come back'.....

Oh know I've made eye contact at least I don't know them I'll have to walk past them 'Have you got the time on you?' *I don't have to answer don't* 'Are you dumb or something?' *Jesus Christ keep walking the corners only a few steps away then this will be in the past* 'Oi I'm talking to you' *I can't answer now I hope they don't follow me I'm bringing it back into the present now by writing this*.....

'I'll take it' *it's not too bad close to town the railway and all that maybe I can get to know these Brazilians I'm staying with who am I kidding that's a lovely warm breeze coming in the back door beats the cold draught at home speak off the cuff go on stop waiting for permission go on speak*.....

Great a job moneys running out just move office furniture easy hope it's not too hot my hands get slippy speak speak how come eve-

Persona Medusa

rybody else is speaking and I am not not again speak there's the harbor bridge for the umpteenth time speak oh do your usual and pretend a genuine laugh at their jokes and funny talk at least there's no meetings to go to in this job imagine me back home going to a meeting it would be about this time.....

Another job unload lorry load of drink great simple manual work pick up box lay it down concentrate don't take for granted that's done what's next oh crap break sit down they're not saying much I won't either.....

Brilliant a job order picking dairy products at night in a cold storage facility I can sleep during the day and leave to work when everyone else is coming in I won't have to hang out with my housemates of an evening wait a minute don't think like this I'm meant to be changing will I speak on the job I know I won't.....

Christmas party how can they be having a Christmas party it's May Jesus Christ I came all this way to avoid a Christmas party at my job at home a boat trip around Sydney Harbour excuse 'Sorry, saving every penny'*.....*

This travelling is bull crap no I'm bull crap get out there and have fun why don't I listen to my own orders to my body do as I say let go time to leave and go travelling I mean leave here and then leave where ever else I go.....

Wish I could stay on this bus Canberra what am I doing here what do you do when you're travelling I'm not really travelling though am I imposter pretender 'Yeah checking in booked over the

◆S4: Blood Trail

phone' *must get some food not canteen in hostel I might have to talk to someone go on outside keep walking there's a pizza place go in there too expensive keep moving there's a café no too cool looking there McDonalds I can do that.....*

Nice pattern comfy carpet nice and warm look out the window now and take in the view like it matters who am I going to tell about a view out the window here's Melbourne I'm really travelling now aren't I 'I fucking hate Backpackers!' *Oh Jesus keep walking keep head down don't make eye contact with him am I heading in the right direction crap.....*

Brilliant Uluru I seen pictures of this in the encyclopedias when younger never even thought of coming over red and blue wish all the images in my head would depart and I could look on this rock now as I did back then 'Excuse me can you take a picture?' 'Of course' *people are nice really now raise my arms* 'Thanks' *wow I just spoke to someone no I asked someone a question and worse for my own benefit Jesus why can't I just shoot nothings into the air and see who picks up on them bloody question like I have to have someone's attention and permission to speak before letting go come on I'm on top of Uluru can't I think of something else.....*

That was a long bus journey there why don't I say that out loud Darwin Jesus Christ man just do something talk to someone stop just walking around that's not travelling there sign for jumping crocodiles do that maybe tomorrow....

Persona Medusa

Ah Cairns I've come a long way haven't I come on now do the Great Barrier Reef I've come all this way for fucks sake yeah there's the sign I'll just go and see the sea maybe tomorrow just keep walking and looking at things shop path sea seats trees people it must be nearly time to leave.....

Sydney again Jesus all that travelling pretend travelling being propelled along on machines and looking out the window I'd better do something before going home ah ah tandem sky dive with video at least it's something 'One skydive ticket please' *oh Jesus here I go adventurer pay attention I don't want to tempt faith by not listening to the safety video right how to express excitement am I excited yeah nervous yeah what to do the noise in this plane is very high I'll just keep quiet* 'You all right?' 'Yeah' 'You're very quiet' *Ah for fucks sake I hate you* 'You're up. Move towards the open door' *get off my back you commentator holy shit this is high I don't want you on my back* 'One, Two, Three, Go' 'Ahhhhh' *keep screaming that's what I'm meant to do who's quiet now eh I want this fucker off my back wait I've stopped screaming start again* 'Ahhhhh' *there's the ground* 'Wow that was brilliant' *do I mean that wait a minute I was only screaming out loud because I was given permission to.....*

Right better go back and change the dates on this ticket she said not to queue and just go straight to her I hate this I would prefer to queue what if somebody thinks I'm skipping the queue and shouts out at me I'd have to respond sometimes I don't all-right just sit down first she's busy with someone wait now too late get her the next time

◀ S4: Blood Trail

now too late now 'Ah you're back. Were you waiting over there?' You must be the quietest person I've ever met' *Noooo what do I have to do I know speak.....*

On a plane again limbo land I don't have to speak here holy shit is that Los Angeles it's fucking huge am I getting out into that oh no look at all them houses and streets and street lights I better not leave the hostel I'd be lost as soon as I'd turn the first corner right check into hostel go to bed I have a good excuse I travelled all night what's all that noise downstairs there's a party down at the bar 'Hey Mate, are you getting up?' 'No I've travelled all night I'm tired' *good excuse what's the point in me going down to a party.....*

That's it nearly home now congratulations I've just managed to travel the world and barely speak to anyone what am I going to do now the least I could have done was get laid what am I going to do about it 'Hey Bro, Have you got the time on you?' 'It's quarter past three' *wow hear the way that New York fireman just spoke free into the free space from that seat over there how did he do that that's brilliant he's off now I'm in a sub way I suppose that's progress should I take the real subway down to the quays to see the statue of liberty no walk I can keep moving and won't have to speak to anyone there I go again that's eighty three streets away just walk.....*

There's Dublin well done I'm a unseasoned traveler now well I suppose I can say I've been here and been there I can lie.....

'I need you to run the site. I need this to work' *Me run a site I've avoided construction sites all my life I need the money though must*

Persona Medusa

tell him I'm capable 'Sure. I'll do that' *what am I doing oh no port a cabins right there's my desk clean up or something ask for a brush go on oh I'll wait go out on site look there's the engineer and foreman and site manager looking into a hole go over to them move ok go go on ok maybe next time into the cabin look at the computer go out-side wait go where what will I look at go on all right don't fall into that trench now walk up along it look at the stone them diggers are big here's the boss coming towards me* 'I told you to tell me what has been used and what should have been used' *what does he mean right back to the cabin onto the computer what's that noise Jesus the neighboring cabin is up in the air right lunch time get up and go into the lunch cabin I have to go on right in* 'D'ya want some brown bread. Me Ma made it last night' 'Yeah, well if you're sure' 'Sure isn't it better than giving it to the dog' *that was good craic right walk around the site talk to people stop walking away from people go towards listen to me stop walking away oh no here's a work mate walking towards me his eyes are down he's not making eye contact it's begun again they know is this I where'd that digger come from fuck right back to the cabin* 'There he is now The Voice of Construction' 'Only speak when you're spoken too' 'Ha Ha Ha' *they're dead right to rile me they've got good loud voices oh no here's the boss bulling towards me* 'DJ I need to speak to you for a minute' 'This isn't working out you're just not vocal enough'.....

There might be money under the couch no shit what do I do three days left until dole day lay on the floor oh my stomach there's that

◆ S4: Blood Trail

eating swirling spiraling jagged edge feeling again I need a job again work in a shop no have to speak to people work in a cinema no have to speak to people work in a bar no work in an office no what can I do that I don't have to speak to people I want to but I can't.....

'When can you start?' 'Monday' *Don't screw this one up speak speak speak at least I know how to cut and paste now.....*

Don't just let other people in the room speak and I sit here saying nothing turn around no don't say something now when staring at the computer 'Here' 'What's that?' 'It's the phone bill' 'What about it?' 'You need to cut back on the calls' 'Fuck You' *holy shit there's a fight on stand back the two MDs are going at it wow I might have a chance here now back to the computer.....*

Oh my God the drink is working again just float over them railings there and tap that girl on the shoulder she won't be expecting it 'Would you like to meet again....?' 'Anita'.

■ S5: Home

There's a dark bowl below me. I am being pulled down to it. The pull down feels like a feather tickling my toes. I can't let go. I can feel the tickling spreading up my legs and into my torso. It is like a bird coming up from the dark, wrapping me in its wings and pulling me down to its nest.

I can hear a phone ringing. I look around the black space. In the distance I can make out a shape. I concentrate on this and suddenly I am there in front of it. There is a red figure behind three big red phones. One phone is ringing. The figure lets it ring. The ring gets faster and faster. The figure picks up the phone. 'Hello'. No answer comes from the other end. It says hello again. Again no answer. It puts the phone down. The second phone rings. It rings faster and faster. It picks it up and again no answer. The third one rings. The first one rings. The second one rings. All three ring together. No answer. I try to call out. I can't. It is like the bird has reached in and plucked out my throat and voice box and now holds them in front of me like a dangling wriggling worm. I reach and thrash for it as I try to scream.

I let go and drop. I turn my head back up. I can see my head up above still spinning with the same thoughts *what time is it my money is running out I should take off my jacket speak do I shake her hand when I leave is this working* They seem as passing leafs in a breeze from down here. I look into the dark pool of tranquility in my pelvic basin. In the pools reflective surface I can see the trail of vertebrae

❧S5: Home

that have led me down to here. Emerging from the dark I see a tiger pouncing silently from one vertebra to the other. Each vertebra it launches from becomes dislodged and falls down in front of me. They each hit the water with a loud splash. I lap up the waters that are thrown over me. The pool bubbles and ripples. I feel the tiger's hot breath on the back of my neck. He comes around and sits beside me. I put my arm around him. His tongue is out. He is panting. I feel his fur. I feel his breath. I feel my pelvic basin fill with vibration. I feel my diaphragm vibrate. I feel my chest vibrate. I feel my mouth vibrate. I open my mouth and ……

Clap. Clap.

Persona Medusa

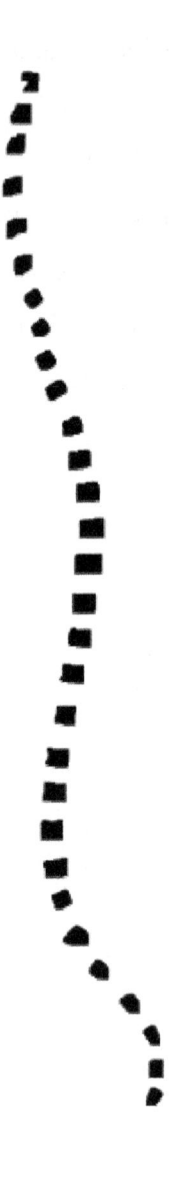

S5: Home

Persona Medusa

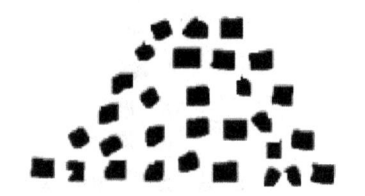

◀ S5: Home

Persona Medusa

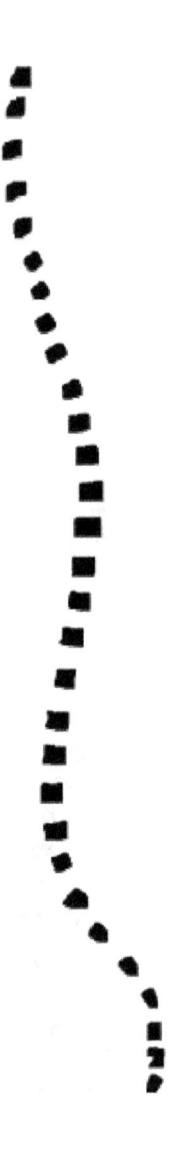

✎ C1: Tale End

The day of the wedding was approaching fast. There was still the option of not giving a speech. There were still the two conflicting snapping voices in my head. *I want to* and *really you I'm still here you know all that therapy crap hasn't got rid of me.*

As a compromise between the two conflicting voices we decided to have the speeches before the dinner. At least with the speech out of the way we could enjoy the dinner. I still expected that jumping crocodiles' mouth clamped on my voice as soon as I began. *Imagine.*

Time passed by as it always does despite my best efforts to hold and appreciate each passing moment before my expected death. Between the dread clouds though there was a glint of light. *So what, I'm actually looking forward to this.* This had attached to it a lovely warm feeling.

I took the mike and stood up. The few drinks I had before hand did not do me any harm. The event manager had advised me to pick a spot on the back wall and speak to that. I began.

'Ladies and Gentlemen, you are all very welcome and thanks for coming'

The microphone picked up my words. I heard them loud and clear throughout the room. I was in command. The confidence of the first word fed back into me in a circular loop and fed into the second.

Persona Medusa

'I'm kind of getting used to this public speaking thing, last week I gave a presentation for my creative writing class titled, 'The History of Weddings - From Cave Men to Present Men'

That sounds stupid did I really write that? Keep going. My voice sounded good.

'And I would like to take this opportunity to let Anita know that I will always strive to be at least one step ahead of the Cave Man'

The guests laughed. It felt great. The good feeling continued on the loop.

'You know these weddings are hard work. One of the good things about being a man in this situation is that they just seem to organize themselves. A toast to Anita for all her hard work in organizing this day'

Another laugh. I was on a high.

'Anita, you're beautiful, smart, funny, kind, a small bit on the short side but sure that's something I can overlook'

You're trying to be too smart you're going to fall on your butt here. Another laugh. The good loop continued.

'Seriously though, Anita tells me that her Grandmother used to be a trader on Moore St in Dublin. I have to say I'm delighted now in some small way to be connected to what was Dublin in the Rare Auld Times'

I got a huge roar from the Dublin crowd and claps all around. I felt great.

C1: Tale End

'I'd like to thank my parents for all they did in raising me and very welcoming Anita in to the family'

'Id like to thank Anita's family for being very welcoming and for giving me a few lessons in Dublinese'

'A toast to the Bridesmaids who all look beautiful in their new red dresses'

'A toast to the groomsmen for all their help, they also look beautiful in their black suits'

A big round of applause for the flower girls who did a great job today'

'And thanks to the hotel for laying on this fine spread today'

'Have a good night'